~THANK GOD FOR CAMOUFLAGE~
(A HEALING IN THE MAKING)

by

Sharon D. Campbell

Edited by: Anthony Ambrogio

Cover Design: James A. Thigpen Jr.

Published by G Publishing, LLC
P. O. Box 24374
Detroit, MI 48224

ISBN 13: 978-0-9843426-3-1
ISBN 10: 0-9843426-3-X

Library of Congress Control Number: 2010901561

Printed in the United States of America

~ACKNOWLEDGEMENTS~

Because this book was spiritually inspired, and since I know that such inspiration is a portion of my purpose in life, I want to first acknowledge the Holy Spirit for its prompting.

I would like to acknowledge my husband, Kenneth, who is the love of my life. I thank him so much for his patience. I thank him for allowing me to go through my season of healing so that I can be a better wife to him and more of a blessing to our children.

I would also like to thank my children for forgiving me and understanding that my lack of parenting was because I had not been freed from the bondage of my past.

I say "Thank you" to the people in my life who have been transparent about the issues that affected their lives. Their spiritual boldness has helped me with my own and allowed me to know that the important thing is my representation of Christ.

My church family at New Beginnings Ministries has definitely played a significant role in my healing process. Apostle Clarence Lewis, Pastor Barbara Lewis, and the other associate Ministers are incredible leaders, and I have learned so much from all of them. Several relationships that I have developed at New Beginnings have indirectly helped me through their teachings and shared experiences, and I am so honored to have had the privilege to glean from them.

The key person that the Holy Spirit used to unlock the door to my healing was Dr. Lydia E.B. Lewis. She has been an awesome leader in the success of my healing. She allowed the Holy Spirit to use her in the most compassionate way, and I appreciate her endurance and consistency throughout the sessions in which she ministered to me. I will always remember her patience in helping me, one of God's struggling children in total bondage, to get back into position and be used by the Holy Spirit.

~CONTENTS~

~INTRODUCTION~

This book is about sexual abuse, a subject that is very familiar to most families. If it has not affected you or your immediate family, more than likely you know someone who has been scarred from it. It is a curse that has been around for centuries, and I am sure that several people have passed through this life who were never healed, never released from the bondage of sexual abuse.

This book is also about a death that I want to celebrate: the death of the darkness that the enemy wanted me to stay in. It is about the light of the Holy Spirit that allows me to walk a new way and have a new way of thinking and being.

As a result of the tremendous healing process depicted in this book, I have experienced a major change in my life. I will candidly take you step by step through my personal journey—a very serious journey with a humorous twist.

My primary goal in writing this book was to assist in my own personal healing. The writing process has helped me to totally empty out, become transparent, and strive to be free and available to the Holy Spirit for refilling.

My prayer is that this book will bless others and encourage them to know that God is unfailing, and, if we allow Him space in our lives, we will know that we are already healed. There is so much tangible assistance available that can connect us to the ultimate healer, Jesus Christ.

I pray that my family will understand that this book is not a personal attack. I want them to know that I love them dearly and living for Christ is the driving force that encourages me to come out of darkness and into His marvelous light. (I Peter 2:9)

~IN A BEGINNING~

In a beginning, God created Sharon Denise Campbell. I was Southern born (in Columbus, GA) and Northern raised (in Flint, MI). My parents were married in 1962, and I came along in 1965 after a brother before me in 1963. Other siblings appeared later. Shortly after I was born, Mom and Dad moved the family north to Flint, MI, to live what everyone thought was the "Good Life" thanks to the General Motors Corporation and its chain of assembly plants for automobiles.

The economy started declining over the course of my youth, and jobs became scarce. Needless to say, the plant that my Dad worked for eventually closed in later years, and the building was demolished. After that, many people started moving back south.

Mom worked at party stores most of her career. Even while working full time, she always had a side hustle going on. She sold jewelry, Tupperware, Mary Kay, Avon, and some other products. She did not want to ask anyone for anything, and she believed in having her own private stash of cash—a stash not even my dad should know about.

She took care of our material needs. I would say that we had more than the average family had at that time because Mom made sure that we had more than what we needed most of the time. Mom was definitely a bargain shopper. She was not into name brands or top-of–the-line attire, but she knew how to put pieces together so that we would look as good as other children. We were always neat and clean, even if our attire was purchased at the local Good Will store. We had nice cars; I even had a brand-new sports car to be shared with my older brother before I even had a driver's license.

She was the authority figure in the home. She was definitely the disciplinarian. She once gave me a whipping because I tore a pair of tights while I was out playing.

That's because she was somewhat of a perfectionist when it came to how we represented ourselves. It was important to Mom how people viewed us, so she would always make sure that we were not going to embarrass her. Mom always emphasized appearance. I remember how tightly pulled my ponytails were because Mom wanted my hair to stay neat all day. Even if we were not going out of the house, we had to get up and get dressed. She would always say, "What if a fire broke out and you had to leave the house in a hurry? You should always get up and get dressed right away." There was no

THANK GOD FOR CAMOUFLAGE

lounging in your pajamas while mom was in the house!

Mom only had one sister in Flint; most of her family was still in Georgia, so that caused her to focus a lot on our immediate family.

Mom was not very affectionate, though. Well, she wasn't very demonstrative in her affections. I guess she thought she would mess up my hair or wrinkle my clothes if she showed too much love. When I was little, I don't remember her ever saying that she loved us kids, but usually we would just know that she loved us by her actions.

Sometimes I would wonder if her actions were more for her satisfaction than for ours because it was usually about how our appearance affected her representation. The way we were raised taught me a lot about how Mom was raised. Thankfully I knew she loved me because of the provisions she made for us, but, as I grew older, I realized the importance of *telling* people you loved them.

Dad's presence in the home was a whole different story. He was definitely the primary bread winner. Working at the assembly plant allowed him to be a good financial provider. He financed most of the household and family needs. Dad did not play a very active role in our lives. He was in the home physically, but there was no emotional attachment. He was an excellent provider financially, but it all filtered through Mom. Dad brought home the bacon, and Mom cooked it up and distributed it out.

My dad was a man of very few words. I don't remember even having a five-minute conversation with him during my childhood. He was very mild mannered. He rarely raised his voice, and he was never in a hurry for anything, but there was one time in my life when my Dad spanked me and my brother real good! My brother got hold of my Dad's shotgun and wanted to play cops and robbers. Well, the gun just happened to be loaded, and I was the robber being chased. Thank God the gun didn't go off, and surely I wasn't going to tell about that dangerous game! Dad later found out about it, and both of us got a pretty serious beat-down. I simply got in trouble for not telling. Cops and robbers wasn't even my game choice; I was scared to death at the time, but, since I wanted to stick with my brother and keep it a secret, I had to stick right beside him for that beating as well. That was the worst whipping ever! Afterwards, my dad took us by one arm and literally threw us onto the bed. I remember wondering if gun-shot wounds would have hurt less. I'm sure that, if that type of whipping occurred today, we would definitely have foster parents!

I also remember Dad being pretty active outside of the home. He was a part of a local

THANK GOD FOR CAMOUFLAGE

motorcycle club, and he and Mom were members of an RV club. He was pretty close to my grandmother, his Mom, so he hung out at her house a lot as well. He and my Uncle seemed to be quite close; my Uncle lived with my grandmother at that time.

Dad enjoyed drinking alcohol. As a young child, I didn't think it was a problem because my Dad was so laid back. When you think of alcoholics, you think of bad tempers, violence, and loud mouths, but my Dad was none of that. Now that I am older and much wiser, I know that a lot of the family members were alcoholics. My Dad just had a cool way of handling his alcohol. He was able to be very functional when he was intoxicated.

My Dad was very reserved, so often times he was taken for granted. I'd never known my dad to bother anyone, but everyone has limits. I am not exactly sure what my Uncle was doing to my Dad on this particular day, but my Dad got up from the table and proceeded to beat my uncle badly, almost as bad as he did my brother and me. My uncle probably didn't feel much that day because he was so drunk. Nevertheless, he ended up on the dining-room floor. I'm sure that he experienced the full effect of the beating the following day as he sobered up.

The unique thing about the fight was that it was the fastest I had ever seen my Dad move.

No words were exchanged; it was a very quiet fight, and, when it was over, my Dad sat back at the table as if nothing had happened. I was about six years of age at this time.

I remember so vividly my Dad getting out of his truck to come in the house from work. It was pouring down raining, and my dad used to park on the street in front of the house. He proceeded to walk up the driveway as if it was a clear and sunny day with no rain in sight!

I used to think something was wrong with him! He would also pull a rabbit out of his hat from time to time and surprise people. There was definitely something different about that whole side of the family, but at the time I didn't know what it was. I couldn't put a word to it at such a young age. Major dysfunctions are the two words that come to mind today.

Mom used to say that my brother and I were the black sheep in the family, and I never really understood what that meant—that is, until years later. We were not sad, pitiful, or lacking, and I guess that was not popular with my family back in the day. We didn't have a bond with either side of our family. We didn't get Christmas or birthday gifts from Grandparents, Aunts, or Uncles. We rarely received visits from family members, and we didn't visit them much either. It was always said that we thought we were better than the rest of the family. It must have

THANK GOD FOR CAMOUFLAGE

been a sin back then to have a good job and live in a nice neighborhood. We lacked a lot emotionally and spiritually, but we always had tangible things.

Mom did not seem to be fed up with the issues in the family, so she decided to expand the family. Along came the birth of another brother in 1971. I didn't understand why Mom felt the need to have this child because she had a boy and a girl already.

I was the baby and the cutest. It seemed to me that the family was complete. I went on to accept this little boy because he was almost as cute as I was. He had very distinctive hair. He had a lot of it, but it would not lie down; it would always stick straight up.

I didn't remember interacting with him much. I'm sure that Mom probably thought he was too young for me to be handling. Still, I started getting excited about being a big sister. As I continued to boss my older brother around, I could look forward to bossing my little brother around as well.

I don't remember being jealous of my brother; I always wanted to help Mom with him. He wasn't around long, though; I remember very clearly the day that he disappeared. He was only a few months old. One day as I was coming home from school, I saw an ambulance and a couple of police cars at my house. I went in the house and went upstairs to his room. I can still picture his dark lips and dark fingertips as the paramedics tried to revive him. My little brother disappeared after that day. I was traumatized! At six years of age, I thought that they would come and get me next. I was a good girl for quite a while after that. No one ever sat me down to explain what happened. I just thought that, if I was really good, I would not disappear like my little brother.

I don't remember the funeral at all. My last vision of my little brother was him lying dead in his crib. That sticks in my mind until this day!

I later learned that my brother died of Sudden Infant Death Syndrome (Crib Death). I'll never forget that horrible day. I was left so confused! My parents just weren't good when it came to teaching their children about difficult life occurrences.

About six months after my brother died, we moved. To me, it seemed as if we moved after only a few weeks, but that was because of my six-year-old's sense of time. We moved to the city of Mount Morris, which, at that time, was an area where Caucasian people predominantly lived. It wasn't a problem for me, but I'm sure that our family members must have really thought that we thought we were beyond them once we moved. We were moving on up to the North side.

THANK GOD FOR CAMOUFLAGE

I was young, naïve, and laid back like my Dad, so quite a few things went over my head. My parents had it going on in my mind; we were progressing!

It was summer time, school was out, and, out of necessity, we had to spend a lot of time at Grandma's house. Her house was located down the street from where my Mom worked. We had a pretty decent time at Grandma's. Being kids, we didn't realize a lot of things, and, for the most part, we thought we were safe there. We thought the way our family was functioning was normal. We didn't realize that we were practically raising ourselves in the midst of so much dysfunction. Alcoholism and all types of discord were prevalent in the house.

After another couple of years, Mom tried to have a child again. It was another brother—lucky me. My brother was born in March of 1973. I was eight years old and determined to be his second mother. I remember thinking that he was going to disappear like my other brother, but he made it, thank God. We have a good relationship now; we joke a lot. When I was older, I would tell him that I begged Mom not to have an abortion, and that was the only reason that he was here. I'll probably be the reason why he'll be in counseling soon!

Mom stayed home for a while with my baby brother, but she soon went back to work.

My grandparents, Big Mama and Big Daddy, continued to care for us while Mom and Dad worked.

Well, things were starting to get a bit weird at Big Mama's house. My Uncle wanted to have private time in the basement with me. It started out with kissing. I vividly remember those times because of the stench from the cigarette smoke when he would stick his tongue in my mouth. That was new to me. I wondered if this was a normal thing that went on in other families.

I was clueless; I didn't believe that my Uncle would hurt me, so I became accustomed to it happening. It never seemed quite right to me, though. I was never comfortable with it. I learned to tolerate it. I didn't fear any physical harm, but I didn't realize the emotional devastation it would cause in my future.

Well, soon after, we started advancing beyond kissing. My uncle started to bring Vaseline to his party and now he was pulling this big thing out of his pants and trying to put it in me from behind. Well, that really didn't seem right, either; he was starting to hurt me. Surely he didn't think that he could put that whole thing inside of me!

He's my uncle, we are family!

I thought that maybe I would become accustomed to that as well. I thought it wouldn't

THANK GOD FOR CAMOUFLAGE

hurt so badly once I got used to it; my thinking was stinking at that time. I was always told that a child should stay in a child's place; something wasn't right; this couldn't be a child's place because there was an adult here!

I remember my Uncle always making a point to tell me that I should not tell anyone about what we did together, and he made his point quite strongly. After all, he was an authority figure, and he was able to discipline me. I remember being quite intimidated. *Maybe I should do what he says*, I thought. I was really trying to figure that thing out!

Well, as the abuse went on and on, I started to realize that he must have had something to lose because he was not telling anyone either, and he always had to sneak around to do what he was doing to me. I thought he might get in trouble if his mother and father found out. Well, since I wasn't liking what he was doing to me but was scared of what he might do if I told, I would just make sure that, when I was in the house, I'd stay near one of my intoxicated grandparents and not give him the opportunity to get me alone in the basement. Hey, that worked pretty good! From that point on, I was always mindful to not be alone with my uncle when he was in the house. I wouldn't even make eye contact so he couldn't beckon for me to come with him to the basement.

Now that it was over, I would just pretend as if it had been a bad dream. I was finally awake, and I didn't ever want to fall asleep again. How do you tell someone something like that anyway, especially with a child's limited vocabulary? I really didn't know exactly what was going on. We were pretty sheltered kids and were never talked to about sex or sexual abuse. I just decided to ignore it.

A couple of years had gone by, and my older brother was old enough to stay home alone with me and my baby brother. Maybe I wouldn't even have to see my uncle again. I never bonded with him or his parents, anyway. They were usually drunk and arguing with each other, so I would really be okay with not seeing them again. *I'll just go on as if they never existed.*

I was living well in denial at that point, and I was safe at home with my family. My secret was safe with me, and I was moving forward very ignorantly.

I couldn't see how men could serve any purpose in my life, so I would just pretend they didn't exist, either—excluding my two brothers, of course.

I thought I was moving to the next phase of life and that things would be better—and then one of my male cousins spent the night. It seemed pretty harmless until he came crawling into my bedroom on his hands and knees. I acted

THANK GOD FOR CAMOUFLAGE

as if I were sleeping. I wasn't really sure what his intentions were, and I was not trying to find out. All I knew was that there were other rooms to play hide and seek in, and I was not going to be the one that he was seeking; I was trying to sleep! One of my parents got up to go to the bathroom, and that startled my cousin and caused him to crawl back out of my room. I wondered if I had some kind of scent that caused the family men to be drawn to me. I thought all men were crazy at that point!

I guess the abuse from my uncle was just not enough. I needed just a little more drama in my life to break me all the way down, as if I wasn't traumatized enough.

After a couple of months had passed, I was home in my bed and minding my own business. I woke up thinking I was urinating on myself. I felt a very warm sensation and thought I should get up and go to the bathroom before I totally wet the bed. I opened my eyes, and I froze when I realized that it was my Dad between my legs and putting his mouth where it shouldn't have been.

Oh my goodness, this is not happening to me! I was literally paralyzed with fear and pretended to be asleep as I tried to figure out whom to address my questions to. Well, my Dad was one of the biggest authority figures in my life, and, at that point, I wasn't sure if Mom was awake because I didn't know what time it was. The first few questions I asked myself were, "Where is my Mother, and doesn't she realize that her husband is not in their bed? Can she not feel that something is not quite right in the house? How long should I lay here and pretend to be sleeping before I check my Dad and put him out of my room? What exactly am I doing to draw this type of attention? Is this the weird stuff that went on in everybody's family? "Has my Dad been talking to my uncle, and this is just a continuation of what my uncle started? Who should I turn to?"—because at 10 years of age, parents are God.

I needed to know what was going on! I don't know if Calgon existed or not at that time, but I definitely needed something or someone to "take me away," like their commercials said! Child Protection Services would have been my best friend had I known about them.

I figured out the safest thing to do. I didn't think I was brave enough to confront my Dad at 10 years old. I still had some fear of him, so I started moving around as if I was just waking up and did not have any feeling between my legs. It worked, and my Dad quickly left the room.

I was really mad after that incident. As soon as the opportunity presented itself, I was going to see what my mom thought about the matter. It had to be wrong because my Dad was

THANK GOD FOR CAMOUFLAGE

married to my Mom, so why was he messing with me? Did he do that stuff to my Mom?

At least my uncle didn't have a woman in his life, and I later found out why. He was an alcoholic who had been physically abusive to his previous wife. *What is up with this male species?*

I was really confused then. I needed sex-education classes and a phone number to law enforcement a.s.a.p. I needed to be informed about how there are sick people in the world—even in a person's family—and that I would have a jacked-up life ahead of me.

I finally got the opportunity to tell Mom what happened. I was determined not to let this go on as long as it had with my Uncle. Of course, I couldn't tell her exactly what happened because I didn't have the vocabulary; I didn't even know that what my Father had done was called oral sex, so you can imagine what my description was like. But, in my mind, my Dad just being in my bed while I was in it should have been enough to get him in trouble—never mind what he was doing!

I had never had the birds-and-the-bees talk. I was clueless about sex and so many other things, so I worked with what I had. I finally told Mom that Dad was in my room and was touching me with his mouth in my private area.

I really didn't get the reaction that I thought I should have gotten. My Mom tried to make excuses for my Dad. I figured it would not have even mattered if I told her about my Uncle, so I didn't. I really thought that I could get everything off my mind and my Mom would handle the rest. I remember asking myself why my Dad wasn't packing his bags to leave our home.

I felt so alone and unprotected. At 10 years old, I didn't have anyone but myself. I remember how my Mom took up for my Dad. She told me that he had been drinking and maybe someone had put something in his drink at the club. "You know he falls asleep anywhere, and you can't trust people," she said. Well I could definitely relate to that one! You can't even trust your parents! I was ready for some new ones at that point! I needed to just start over with a whole new family!

My Mom's solution was to put a lock on my door so that I could lock it at night when I went to bed. I was ready to lock the whole world out, including her. It was the most abandoning feeling ever; my parents—my gods—had failed me!

That was the "official" opening of my can of worms, my Pandora's Box—the start of my childhood dilemmas, my life issues. The root cause of why I am where I am today, struggling to deal with what I have created within myself. I am bound by events that I was never taught to deal with, allowing matters to spill over into every aspect of my life and thinking that this is the way that God would have it be; this is how God made me. It was a devastating awakening when I found out differently thirty years later.

~IN THE MEANTIME~

I am cruising through life without a clue. I am faking it through the rest of elementary school and, looking back, I realize that I used my sense of humor as the tool to camouflage my issues. It actually worked out pretty well. I had developed lots of friendships, but the humor allowed me to keep my friends from getting too close to me. They never knew if I was serious or not, so they usually didn't try to get too deep into my business. It didn't keep them from telling me their business, though. I guess they saw something in me that I was trying not to see in myself because I had to protect my own stuff. I was very personable and an excellent listener. Even in the midst of acting silly, I would always take time to listen.

I took pride in making people laugh. I was very compassionate, and I remember always wanting everybody to be happy. No one should hurt on the inside like me. I thought I would just devote my life to saving everybody in the world from their issues. After all, no one should have to be alone with not even their parents to protect them.

THANK GOD FOR CAMOUFLAGE

I thought I'd try something new, so I started attending church. I had heard that church people were pretty cool. *I guess it's worth a try*, I thought: *I might have to deal with actual human beings in some capacity at some point in my life.*

We lived across the street from a preacher, so I went to church with him and his family. I used to go alone because Mom rarely went when I was growing up. I don't remember my Dad ever going to church, not one time. I continued on my own just as I felt I had been most of my little life.

Mom said that she was forced to go to church frequently as a child, and, when she left her Mom's house, she started doing her own thing. I, on the other hand, always loved to go to church once I got started. I always felt safe there. I didn't think church people would let anyone hurt me. Church folk always seemed to be genuine; they were encouraging, and they seemed to love me even though they knew nothing about me. They didn't seem to want anything from me.

I was always a bit uncomfortable with too much attention because I didn't want people to find out about my secrets, and I wondered if there were any strings attached if they tried to get too close. I didn't want to slip up and allow my problems to become apparent because, at that stage in life, when I was approximately 11 years old, I was working on my coping and defense mechanisms. I needed to figure out how to act to pull off this camouflaging thing. So much of what I went through I brought upon myself. Looking back, I can see how sad it was that I was not directed differently.

Anyway, this particular church that I was visiting was a bit overwhelming for me because there were things going on that I did not understand. People were speaking in weird languages and not in control of their body movements. Some people even fell unconscious, and nobody called the paramedics; it was a bit scary, so eventually my visits started to lessen. No one in my family was spiritually equipped to explain the details of church and denominations, so I continued trying to figure things out on my own.

I'm 12 now, and I just can't seem to understand why my Dad is still living in the house with us. It has to be my fault; no one else is being held accountable. Anything bad that happens to me is somehow because of me. That is what I chose to believe at the time. I guess I should be thankful that there was only one incident with my Dad; the lock on my door nipped that in the bud quickly. I wish I would have told on my uncle sooner; maybe I could have gotten a lock put on the basement door at Big Mama's house as well. I figured I should just get over it and

THANK GOD FOR CAMOUFLAGE

move on because nothing good would have come out of it anyway.

Soon, I was cruising through the 7th grade, and boys were starting to become more interesting to me. I was hoping to attract some boys my age who were not relatives. I was still quite clueless about life because of the environment that chose me. I still hadn't had the sex talk; I had not been taught about sexually transmitted diseases, teenage pregnancy, menstrual cycles, or anything else I needed to know. I had not even been taught about Salvation, but I had been getting a bunch of misinformation from my uneducated peers in school.

I remember my first menstrual cycle. I went to the bathroom and discovered that my underwear were a different color than when I put them on, so I called my Mom to the door and told her that I thought I had started my period and I needed her to go to the store and get me some protection. The store was really close to our home, so I stayed in the bathroom while she went and got the sanitary pads. She brought them to the bathroom door, and not another word has been said about it to this day. Mom was very uncomfortable with a lot of things that she should have been teaching her children, but she did the best she could with the knowledge that she had.

During this time, I continued to go to church on occasion with neighbors and friends. I really didn't know what I was looking for or why I always felt the need to go. I knew that there was something for me at church, but, since I didn't know about the importance of God in my life, I was still wandering around in my personal wilderness, trying hard to get home.

In the midst of my wilderness, Mr. Right managed to find me, and I really liked him; it was true love. This was the one who would take me away from all of my brokenness, and it wasn't Jesus. I liked this boy so much that I thought I was ready to have sex. I had learned quite a bit from my peers who were sex experts in junior high. I planned my first sexual experience at 13. Needless to say, it was overrated, unfulfilling, and never should have happened. It was too soon and not the road I should have been traveling.

That was the first sexual experience that I had consented to, and I really should have passed on that opportunity as well. I'm sure that it was very embarrassing for him because, when he was done, I had the nerve to ask him if that was it. I thought I would see fireworks and fall deeper in love and we would run off into the sunset—and then I remembered that was a television show with a bunch of actors. I just wanted him to run away from my house by himself and not look back! It was yet another

THANK GOD FOR CAMOUFLAGE

unfulfilling sexual experience. My peers had misled me! I probably should have just become a nun and lived a sex-free life right at that moment. *Sex is overrated*, I thought.

I had completed my fourteenth year of life; December had arrived, and the excitement in my life continued. All was camouflaging well; I was faking it until I could make it in life, and I started looking forward to Christmas day. I usually got most of what I wanted for Christmas. We lived a pretty good life, and we didn't lack much as far as material things were concerned, so I was expecting big things.

On December 2, 1979, my Dad was killed in a tragic accident. He was hit by a train while driving across the railroad track. I still have not figured that one out yet, because my Dad was such a reserved person, and I could not imagine him trying to beat a train; I had never known him to even drive the speed limit. He hung out all the night before, and that particular morning the sun was very bright. Maybe he just didn't see the blinking red lights, and, since there were no rails at this particular railroad crossing, maybe he blindly proceeded to drive across. That's all I could come up with. Who really knows?

I remember my Mom calling home from the hospital after having to identify my Dad's body and casually saying, "Your Dad is dead." I remember thinking, *Can't you break it to me gently? Don't you want to know if I am alone or not? Shouldn't I be sitting down? Couldn't you have waited until you got home?* The way she revealed it to me was just so shocking! Her teachings while she was growing up must have been truly lacking, somewhat like mine. I don't even know if I responded the correct way. I asked her what happened, and I told her that I would see her when she got home from the hospital. I don't even remember crying. I was just numb at that point. Why did I allow my family to just throw me off-track like that? I really should've expected just about anything from them.

Anyway, now Mom was planning a funeral just a few weeks before Christmas. This was not a good gift—definitely not the type of big thing I'd been expecting. I did not want my Dad in the house, but I never wished him dead. I wasn't distraught about losing my Dad because I really did not know him that well. We never had that father-daughter bond.

I remember not wanting to go to the funeral because there would be too much attention on the family and too many people in my face. I always thought that someone would sense what had been going on with me. I lived in constant fear of that. I was somewhat paranoid at times. I could not get out of going to the funeral, so I tried to get out of going to the wake;

that didn't work either. I managed to endure them both.

It was over; I did not have to lock myself in my room anymore; and I could sleep more peacefully. Thank God there were no problems with my brothers sexually abusing me.

Three years passed, I was 17. My Mom remarried, providing me with a stepfather. I really hoped that I would not have to go through any changes with this man because now I had gained a little knowledge about abuse, not to mention some attitude, and I was old enough to leave that place if I had to. I didn't know where I would go, but I would have protected myself and I would not have thought twice about relocating. I was not taking any more abuse! It was all about me then.

My stepfather seemed to be a nice man, and I was trying hard not to prejudge him, but I always kept an eye on him just in case. It turned out that Mom was still the dominant personality in the house, so I really did not have many dealings with him personally. He had two children, and the three of them moved in with us. My stepdad rented out the home he previously lived in. His son was a few years older than me, and we did not have a lot in common; we did our own thing. His daughter was younger. She had a couple of issues—she was spoiled and undisciplined—but she grew out of most of it.

Usually, our house was pretty normal. We had a few personality challenges here and there, but we made it through. I'm sure it could have been worse than it was, but everything worked out. I think all of us just had to get used to a new way of living with more people in the home.

A year passed, and I had gone through lots of dysfunction in my life. I had an abortion; I dropped out of school after receiving a scholarship to a major university. I got married in 1984. I got pregnant again in 1985, I kept this child, and, shortly after that, I was in the midst of a divorced and back at home.

Being back at home with a child was a very humbling experience for me. I had to endure six months there while saving for a security deposit on an apartment. I finally got my own place and thought I was on my way.

I met my second husband and married again in 1988. I buried a child while I was with him in 1990 and had another child in 1992. I was still hanging on to issues and allowing them to infest most of my life. I was 28 years old with two kids and on my second marriage. Nobody could tell me that I didn't have life all worked out.

I was independent, and could do what I wanted. Although I had not mastered that submissive stuff, I had some training from Mom on how to dominate a household. I battled

THANK GOD FOR CAMOUFLAGE

constantly with doing what was right as opposed to being a product of the environment that I was raised in. My mind was in turmoil frequently. I was trying to figure out who I was and where I was going in life. I should have figured it out before I got married the first time!

I didn't think much of family at that time, so when my abusive uncle died on January 8, 1993, I was not moved by it at all. His death was no surprise, considering the way he lived. I really did not want to attend his funeral. I was actually relieved about not having to see him anymore and experiencing the discomfort I always felt around him. I had deeply rooted bitterness at that time. I could not stand being around him because of what he had done to me, and, yet, I felt sorry for him because, after his wife left him, he just could not seem to get his life back on track.

After his divorce, he lived with his parents (my grandparents) until he drank himself to death. On the rare occasions that I did see him, I could tell that he was deteriorating more and more. He had lost so much weight, and his skin was getting darker. He started looking like death, even before he died. I remember him cursing my grandparents and telling them where to go and what to suck. I don't know why they allowed him to stay there so long; I'm sure they feared him as they got older.

I thought his suffering on earth and his death was because of what he did to me and how he treated my grandparents. In my mind, he went straight to hell!

His funeral was so sad. It was at the funeral home, of course, because he did not frequent anyone's church. There were only a few people there. He didn't have many friends, and the ones that were there looked just the way he did before his death. I didn't even stay the whole time. I went to show my face because I had to remember that no one knew what he had done to me, so I made an appearance just like a good niece would. It was so cold and dead in the whole room. I felt that I was being sucked up by the dark spirit that dwelled within that place. I remember not shedding a tear and boldly walking out before the service was over.

I thought I was protecting myself at that time in my life. You could not have told me that I was not in complete control. It was just me and me alone.

As cold and bitter as I was about my family, I continued going to church. I needed something that church people had, but I had not figured it out yet. I started going to church with my husband and his family, and later, when mom started going back to church, I ventured off and joined the church that she attended. My husband eventually ended up following so that we could

THANK GOD FOR CAMOUFLAGE

worship together; we were so out of order! I served there for approximately six years, and, during that time, I led a youth group called Acteens. It was an outreach ministry that consisted of girls aged 12 to 17. Acteens is a national organization that was very prosperous at our church. Out of all the churches in our city, we were the only African-American branch.

I recall a couple of incidents when girls would come to me for help because they were being sexually abused by a family member. Even though I was their youth leader, I could not understand why they were coming to me with this type of issue. I could handle anything else, but I was not trying to deal with sexual-abuse issues because I had not dealt with my own. I realized later that these girls coming to me was a case of familiar spirits being drawn to each other.

I also know that it was a spirit that I was not trying to connect with. I did talk one of the girls into sharing with her parents so she could get help. The other girl was a guest and not a consistent participant, so I just brushed her off. I really thought the devil was torturing me with my past. I later found out that I needed to confront my issues so that I would be better equipped to minister to those girls instead of running from them. That was definitely a learning experience for me.

I was in a position of leadership and trying to avoid leading in certain areas. I expected the girls to know what I was uncomfortable with and to take those issues to someone else. I really wanted to help them, but I needed to help myself first. I soon realized that help was on the way!

~INNER HEALING I~

I was 40 years old, in the prime of my life, and I was more than established spiritually, financially, socially, etc. I should have been giving myself a birthday bash where I could greet all of my peers and family members whom I had not seen in years and I should have been standing before them, sharing how awesome my life was and how obedient my children were and how well rounded my husband was: he had an executive position in a top-notch firm and showered me with gifts and love. I should have been expressing how my life could not be more perfect. I should have been sharing how I had traveled around the world twice and how we had homes in five different countries and—oh, what a wonderful life!

Once I awakened from that dream, I realized that self examination had taught me that my life was a hot mess! I can honestly say that it was more of a personal mess than anything having to do with my husband or children.

The world's way of teaching leads us to believe that having lots of money would solve all of our problems. We could buy a new face and a new body. We could buy homes, businesses, and even some people. We could have a healthy body with our personal trainer and personal chef. We could definitely buy some temporary happiness. I've even thought about contacting Oprah a few times to see if we could work some things out financially and I could get a temporary fix of happiness. However, life experiences have taught me that inner peace, obedience, wisdom, self discipline, perseverance, a good attitude, etc., can get you where Oprah is and much farther; I should have called her anyway!

I was in the prime of my life, and I should have been happy, so it was time for me to get out of the way! I was learning more and more about God's love and I really wanted to represent Him. I was in a new season, and I wanted to be pleasing in God's sight. I was determined to do some things differently in my life!

My husband went to his church simply because that was the church that he grew up in. He is very family oriented and wanted to worship with his family. I attended the church of my choice simply because my Mom had finally gotten back in church and I was trying to be family oriented just as my husband was. I had always admired the closeness that he had with his family. I made the best of it while I was at my church, and it was definitely a learning experience, but we were there for all of the wrong reasons. There was no fulfillment, and there was too much religion that did not coincide with the scriptures.

I decided that, since my husband was the head of our household, I needed to allow him to lead us spiritually. We visited different churches for a little while, and I humbly followed where my husband led. We joined a new ministry called "New Beginnings," not realizing that this would literally be a new beginning for us. I was observing and enjoying the love and support from the congregation. I was also enjoying the leadership and the teachings that I was receiving. I loved the fellowship that was shared. I knew that my ministry was with the youth, so I started assisting and helping out in the youth department. I was definitely not looking to lead anything. I was very comfortable in the background. That had always been my comfort zone. I was really trying to learn where the Holy Spirit wanted me to be. There were times when I knew that I should deal with my issues so that I could hear God more clearly. I had been running things and running from things for far too long.

It was time for me to get to work, so I joined the choir, which was my second love. The choir director, who was also one of the associate ministers, seemed to be a good representative of Christ. She was a great director, and she played the saxophone like a pro.

After we had been there for about a year or so, the ministry started Bible-study teachings on Inner Healing, and our choir director was the minister heading those sessions. Shortly after the teachings started, I was spiritually motivated to meet with her privately. I chose not to share in regular Bible study because I was in so much bondage to my issues and couldn't risk being exposed. I would just listen without much expression; it was basically the way I have always been in church: keep your composure; don't let them see you sweat; give the appearance that all is well in your life; do not get too emotional—because I thought expressed emotions could tell everything about a person!

Even though I thought I needed private sessions, I was not really sold on the idea because I still had some insecurities about my lack of a relationship with the minister. We did not have a relationship outside of church, and I just didn't know how personal I wanted to get with her.

Although I had developed a sense of humor early in life as one of my coping mechanisms, I was never a loud, boisterous person. I guess you could call me an undercover comedienne. I would be the one cracking jokes in the background, making people laugh, getting them into trouble, and looking as if I didn't know why they were laughing. The minister had a

THANK GOD FOR CAMOUFLAGE

sense of humor as well, and that was probably why she tolerated me. I believe we were more alike than we realized at that time.

I started to have doubts about whether or not I wanted the minister in my business. I had to see her too often, and she would probably start to look at me differently. I was not sure if she was equipped to separate a person's past from the point that God had brought them to in the present. Was it possible for her to see the potential of my future? I did not want my issues to get in the way of any possible future advancements for me in the ministry because she definitely had influence in the church. I didn't want to be viewed as too fragile to be a vessel for the Lord. I was still unsure about it. I wanted to find out if the Holy Spirit was leading me to go there. This could have been an example of God's sense of humor.

The devil will try any trick in the book to keep us out of the light. He wants us to live in darkness and stay bound so that we cannot have an open relationship with God. He wants us to feel unworthy of God's love and divine healing.

What I'm trying to say is that, even though the minister did have influence in the church, as a woman of God ministering to help God's people, she should have been obedient enough to make a spiritual assessment and allow God to deal with her as she dealt with me.

I was not ignorant of the fact that ministers are not super humans and they too have challenges in their lives, but I would like to believe that those ministers at my place of worship who have challenges are actively dealing with them through the aid of the Holy Spirit. I believe that the ministers at my place of worship, the ones who cover me and my family, are able to separate carnal realities from spiritual obedience.

After fighting with my perceptions of the situation and allowing the devil free reign in my head, I decided to take a chance and open up to the minister. The Holy Spirit says, "Yes, I am leading you to go there!"

Personal Inner Healing began. The minister seemed very willing to counsel me for several sessions on her personal time, so maybe God was leading us to each other.

I typed up sheets on the computer to make myself a home-made journal. I was eager to see my progress and wanted to be able to look back on it. I kept track of how I felt before the sessions, what went on during the sessions, and how I felt after the sessions. I wanted to be able to focus on how far I had come and not on how far I had to go.

Session I: The devil tried to discourage me before the session all the way to the door, trying to get me back to the car; trying to convince me that *It's not worth it; it's only going to cause a bunch of heartache; you've already got enough problems*, but I made it to the door. "I can do this," I said to myself.

I got inside and sat down face to face with the minister. This was very uncomfortable, and I wondered if she would be looking in my face the whole time. I was trying to get through the session with just a little bit of dignity. I proceeded to bare my naked truth, and I tried to summarize what I thought my problem was.

I told her about the things that were forced upon me as a child and how difficult it had been. I was so nervous; *What have I gotten myself into?* I thought. I did not make a lot of eye contact, and I was sure that at times I didn't make a lot of sense either. I hadn't figured out how I wanted to tell her what I wanted to say. As a result, I was going all over the place with my conversation. At one point, I turned my chair away from her because I had a hard time keeping my composure and I didn't want her looking in my face while it transformed into ugliness.

Two of my main goals throughout the sessions were to keep my composure and to stay in control. I learned that it was okay to cry and it's not always a sign of weakness. I had a lot of things to cry about, and, since I rarely cried, I needed to release some years of stuff. The main thing I discovered was that God was and still is the main focus, and I needed to relinquish control and give it to Him so that He could help me through this ordeal. I was really freaking out after this first session. I asked myself if this was really going to be confidential, and I wondered if it would get easier. I didn't know if the minister was ready for me.

I hoped she would not regret helping me. She was really going to take time out of her schedule just for me? Was I that important to her? How would I repay her?

She gave me phone numbers to contact her if I needed her in between sessions. Did she really mean "call at anytime," like a 24-hour service? *I don't know if I can do this!*

Session II: I felt as if I were regressing back to childhood. I did not know that I had to relive everything that I had gone through. I had planned this to be a much smoother transition. I didn't know if I was ready to turn back the hands of time and go back to such a place. The bondage was easier: "Conceal and not deal."

The minister suggested that I find a safe place to go in my mind to be able to tolerate the intense pain. I needed to find a place to rest in the peace of God through meditation. I was having a hard time finding a safe place. I had felt so alone and unsafe for so long, and I had

THANK GOD FOR CAMOUFLAGE

become my own safe place. At that point, I was thinking a safe place would be anywhere other than a therapy session!

The session was still very uncomfortable. I was in a mega battle with myself and my fears. On one hand, I was breaking down and confessing issues and realizing that I was in need of much spiritual guidance, and, on the other hand, I was acting as if I had it all together and was still trying to be in control. A lot of mixed emotions were churning inside of me. I was sure that she thought I was crazy by then!

I had been suppressing this stuff for over thirty years, and I was realizing the hard way that this would not be an overnight success!

I was eventually able to confess that I was really messed up, and that I really needed her assistance in a most urgent way. It was the end of the session, and I was on my way out the door. It was so embarrassing because I was in such a desperate state! I felt like a person who had been thrown in the middle of the ocean and couldn't swim. The minister was my life guard, and I was holding on to her for dear life; it wasn't pretty!

We were meeting twice a week, and it didn't seem like enough. I wanted to move in with her until I could conquer that thing.

I remember an incident after this session when I was driving to work. I pulled into the driveway of my employer and thought I was having a nervous breakdown. I had never experienced anything like it, so I called the minister and asked her what she thought I should do. I could not go in to work until I could get my emotions under control. She said that she would meet with me and help me to get through that episode. Even though I wanted to meet with her with all the little strength that I had at that moment, I started realizing that I was depending on her too much, and I said, "No, thank you." I told her that I would be okay and that I just needed her to pray with me on the phone. I did not want to interrupt her life at a moment's notice to come and rescue me—well, I *did*, but I resisted acting on it.

I was really confused! *How much do I utilize her services and when is it too much? Should I even be contacting her outside of the sessions?* I was feeling extremely needy! I knew what she had said about calling when I needed her, but I wondered if she could be really sincere about her commitment to help me, especially because I was feeling that I must have been more than she had anticipated!

I knew that I was more than *I* had anticipated! I was unsure about so many things in life because I had no stability in my relationship with Christ. Once you know that you know, you are not so susceptible to all of the questions that the devil will throw at you to

THANK GOD FOR CAMOUFLAGE

make you unsure of yourself and about your relationship with God.

The minister provided me with a sheet of scriptures that affirmed who I am in Christ. I was to speak the word of God daily until it was imbedded into my spirit. I wanted to wean myself away from those sessions and the minister. Sometimes I really wished I had paid to go to the Caucasian therapist across town—a male therapist who could not relate to me in any way whatsoever, a person who I would never see outside of therapy. I could go in and spill my guts, be healed and never have to see him again. However, at that point it was too late for what I should have done. I had to be in it to win it. "This Inner Healing stuff is serious business," I said.

Session III: Okay, I had a self diagnosis of compulsive and obsessive behavior. I was becoming very withdrawn from my family, and I was having some trouble functioning throughout a full day. I was becoming more drawn to the minister. She was becoming my little god. It is safe to say that I was adding another issue on top of a pile of issues.

Before this particular session, I wrote the minister a letter to let her know about my concerns of becoming a fatal attraction. This really concerned me because it had always been me against the world up to that point, and I was upset about allowing her into my world. I had been maintaining by myself, and then everything was out of control! I needed to know how to deal with that—quickly.

I had shared more things with her than I had shared with my husband—things that I had suppressed most of my life. I had really opened up for the first time in my life, and now, every time I saw her, I felt so uncomfortable. I tried not to make too much eye contact, and I would limit conversation with her. Usually, I would not say too much to her unless she said something to me. I didn't want to make her uncomfortable just because I was uncomfortable. She probably already had an impression of me as a very fragile person, and that bothered me because I was not generally like that. I was strong in several areas of my life, if you would let me tell it.

What I really wanted to do was to get out of the choir and maybe even leave the church, but I had been running all of my life, and I was tired. I really hoped that I was not offending her or making her think she had done anything wrong. The minister was always mindful of dealing only with the issues and not getting caught up in my carnal responses to my issues. She had always been very consistent in her ministering, but I really did not want to be the one to take her out of the spirit realm and to the point where she would want to do bodily harm to me. I could be the situation to provoke her to wrath. I felt minimum stability during that time in my life, and, at times, I would act out on those feelings. Hopefully I would not mess things up too badly and we would be able to maintain some kind of a friendship after these sessions ceased.

Anyway, I wrote the letter to let her know that I was aware that I was going from one extreme to the other and that I was working on *not* doing that. I didn't want to push her away, and I definitely was not going to start the sessions over with someone else. I didn't want anyone else to know that I had temporarily lost my mind. I started with the minister, and I wanted to finish with her.

There were other times when I would be driving and I would have serious breakdowns. I would have to pull over and pray. Sometimes I would be so exhausted from crying and praying that I would fall asleep in someone's parking lot. I probably could have been doing something just a little bit safer at that time! I was feeling so alone, just as I did when I was a child.

I would sit there hoping the minister would call or drive by and save me. Sometimes I would sit at the minister's place of employment and wait for her to get off work because I needed her assistance. Each time, however, I would come to my senses before it was time for her to get off work, and I would leave so that she would not get a personal-protection order filed against me. I had a little pride left hanging around in the distance.

I was starting to relate to alcoholics, drug addicts, and suicide victims. Some days I wanted some rest temporarily, just to get a break from it all, and other days I could understand why people would just take their lives and have a permanent solution. Of course I couldn't tell many people that I thought that because I would have definitely been admitted somewhere with a straight jacket attached to me. I actually found myself getting caught up in a commercial about depression; I was ready to claim that thing totally! I didn't call the number, but I did check out the website, and I definitely was a strong candidate. I believed I would have been an outstanding spokesperson for depression at that moment.

I was ready to put all of my worms back into the can they came out of because I felt that I needed to go to a rehabilitation center and be on 24-hour watch. I was in a major struggle dealing with all of those years of stuff that had piled up!

This session was actually productive. I got through it without crying; we had good conversation; and I was moving forward. I was a little emotional that evening, just because I was overwhelmed by it all, but I was determined to get through it all.

Session IV: Before this session, I had written another letter to the minister because she had to cancel our previous session. I was very disturbed because I had been anxiously waiting for every session since we started. She did not say why she was canceling, so I assumed she had just put someone else before me. I even thought that she was getting tired of me and just needed a break. *I* was even getting tired of myself at that point.

I went from being independent and doing my own thing to dependent and needing all of the minister's attention. I remember being upset because I was desperate. I hated feeling so needy! I really felt the need to be in control! Why had I allowed this to happen!

She responded so kindly to my somewhat ignorant letter, explaining to me that she had been sick and stayed home to rest.

She also said that in the future she would give clarity if any other sessions needed to be cancelled. Imagine how stupid I felt after that! It was very selfish of me to think that I was the only thing going on in her life. I guess I would have been upset even if she was out spending time with her husband. I think I wanted us to be conjoined twins at that point; she was small enough for me to drag around on my hip. I really needed a clue!

I wrote another letter about my previous letters, and I thought about how comfortable I was with writing. It was a form of expression which allowed me to convey my thoughts with ease; I had a very hard time expressing myself verbally. I was explaining to the minister about how there is so much more power in verbal communication because of words being spoken into the atmosphere. Faith comes by hearing, and hearing by the word of God. I really thought about the word "hearing," and I thought about how God spoke everything into existence; whatever God said, it came to pass. The power of life and death is in the tongue. It has to be put into the atmosphere in order to manifest itself, whether it is spiritual or carnal. I realized that letters can be very descriptive and can benefit you and the person that they are being shared with—but are you really being cleansed and healed if you do not verbally release those things? Is it just as healthy to simply write down your thoughts? I was not sure about that, but I didn't want to make letter writing a crutch. I needed to learn how to communicate with people verbally as well.

This really became clear to me when the minister asked me to write out a Lament to the Lord. She wanted me to write a detailed summary about the sexual abuse and how I really felt about it. She said to be very honest and specific, and she did not want me to worry about the language I used. That was very easy for me. I could do that with no problem. When I finished, she would know exactly how I felt and how all of this chaos was affecting me. This Lament would be for our eyes only, and then maybe we could have a burning ceremony or something.

That was a very comfortable assignment for me. Well, that was until she asked me to read it aloud to the Lord and share with Him exactly how I felt. She wanted me to cry out to the Lord as if I was actually that child experiencing the abuse all over again, as if I was in the room by myself. I could not say that stuff out loud, even if she was not there! I didn't even talk that way normally! I thought I was going to pass out! I was sure that she would read it on her own, briefly elaborate on it, and then we would set it on fire and be done. There was a major difference between writing and speaking! *How am I supposed to help others if I am not comfortable talking about this thing? I can't write letters to everyone who has been sexually abused.*

I still had a few things to work out. I lacked communication skills in regard to this matter; I'd been silent about it for over 30 years!

I managed to read the Lament aloud, totally embarrassed. It was definitely a learning experience.

I hoped I would survive future sessions. This session was very beneficial. We did an exercise that required me to make an outline of my body on paper and to write down, inside the head on my outline, some issues and other negative things that had been instilled in me. On the body of my outline, I started to write all of God's promises and positive things in His word. I surprised myself when I started to flow with that. I did not realize how much of God was in me. I only stopped because I ran out of space. A lot was brought to my attention on that day, and I denounced the bad things. I stood on the promises of God, praying to Him and allowing Him to work it out for me. It was very intense, and it ended up being a two-hour session. Sometimes you need to see yourself outside of yourself, if you know what I mean.

Session V: I was not too anxious before this session. I think I would have been all right if it was cancelled, but I was still looking forward to it. We assessed what we had gone over, trying to make sure that I was having total cleansing, being sure to properly grieve each issue and refill on the word of God. The minister was doing an excellent job of ushering me into the presence

THANK GOD FOR CAMOUFLAGE

of God and allowing Him authority over my life because I had been trying to protect and cover myself for a long time and I had failed in so many areas.

I thought about how I had failed my daughters. I did not allow them their independence. I did so many things for them when I should have been teaching them. My children still need assistance with things that they should know how to do on their own. The best way for them to learn would be for them to do it themselves, but I would always do for them to make sure that it was done right or simply done at all. I did not want to put more on them than they could bear. As they grew older and were allowed to do more things on their own, it was very frustrating for me because I had never taught them properly and would get upset with them if I had to help them—when I should have been upset with myself.

They were very sheltered. There was not much spending the night anywhere. They were always a few years behind what average children were doing because I was in over-protective mode all the time. I would do almost everything for them, and I didn't realize that I was handicapping them.

I recall listening to other parents conversing about their children and sharing how early the kids started washing dishes or washing their own clothes. They would teach their children how to cook and do their own hair, allowing them to do these things until they got them right. My concern was always about preventing waste: "Get it right the first time, or I will do it," I said.

I thought about how I failed my husband by not allowing him to be a total father to our children. I had serious issues with my husband bathing them and changing their diapers when they were babies and toddlers. I was more relaxed once they were old enough to talk and tell me if someone hurt them. I always thought that, if my father and uncle could sexually abuse me, surely my husband had the potential to do the same to our girls! When I was sexually abused, I was too young to know what signs to look for to protect myself, so, in my eyes, if you were a man, you had the potential to be a sex offender. I thought my oldest child had an even greater potential to be abused because she was my husband's step child. I focused on that even more.

I did not want my girls sitting on my husband's lap, and they had to always be properly covered up with clothing. There was absolutely no walking around the house half dressed!

The devil had me thinking crazy sexual thoughts about my husband if I had to leave him

THANK GOD FOR CAMOUFLAGE

home alone with the girls. I clearly remember an incident that happened after my older daughter graduated from high school. My younger daughter was at school, and I was at work. I was on my way home for lunch. I called as I was on my way, and I didn't get an answer. I knew that my husband and daughter should have been there. I called three times in a row, and I did not get an answer. I was so upset; in my mind, I pictured my husband in bed with my daughter, and I started speeding and getting so paranoid that I almost hyperventilated. I walked in the door yelling and screaming about no one answering the phone. I was frantic and wanted to know what the hell they were doing!

My daughter was getting out of the shower and hadn't heard the phone. My husband didn't hear the phone because he was outside on the lawn mower cutting the grass. Imagine how cute that was. I was so embarrassed but too upset to apologize. I couldn't explain why I was so upset or tell them about all of the things that I was thinking because they would have thought I was crazy. The sad part is that I didn't realize how unstable I was concerning the sexual abuse I had experienced. I was prepared to do bodily harm to my husband without any hesitation!

I was so caught up in making sure that my kids didn't experience what I had experienced. I was determined not to be like my mother; I was going to protect my children! I spent most of my time trying to protect them, and I didn't love and nurture them like a good mother would. I was quite a radical about my children being abused, and that caused me to lack in other areas of parenting.

I was never very affectionate toward them. I could do without the hugs and kisses, and it was even okay if they didn't say "I love you." I thought my actions were enough. It seemed that, the more I tried not to be like my Mom in one area, the more I was following her footsteps in another.

My first memory of my Mom saying those words to me was when I was married, pregnant, and thousands of miles away in Hawaii. My Mom would not even come for the birth of her first grandchild; she said that she was not flying over all of that water. I was quite upset about that. I would always say, "No matter where my first grandchild is born, I would definitely be there for support." My Mom taught me so many things not to do with my children.

Anyway, Mom and I were ending our conversation one day, and I really wanted to tell her that I loved her, but I was terrified that she would not reciprocate! I was more afraid of that than I was of saying the actual words myself. I gathered up enough strength to say, "I love you, Mom" and she actually said it back. It was such a relief that I almost collapsed on the floor. It was a good thing, but it was also ridiculous that it was such a challenge for me. No child should have to go through all of those changes to tell a parent that they love them. Life happens in ways that are beyond our control.

I don't have any memory of my Dad ever telling me that he loved me, so I was okay without it. I survived in a very dysfunctional way, but I survived. I guess it's safe to say that I was just longing for someone to genuinely love me; to show just any kind of positive parental love—someone that I could depend on!

My older daughter turned out to be non-affectionate like I was. She reminds me so much of my Mom (and of me), so I was okay with her. It was a generational curse that had slipped up on me and I, in turn, passed it on to her. My younger daughter is very fortunate because she had more genes from my husband's side of the family. I really have to be mindful to this day to respond positively when she is being affectionate with me. Displaying affection with my children was always very uncomfortable for me. I must have subconsciously thought that love and affection toward my children could turn into something bad. Did I have to protect my children from myself? That was my twisted thinking at the time.

As cleansing took place, I started to realize why I did and said certain things. Before the sessions, I really thought that God had made me the way I was. I thought, "I am just a reserved person who likes to stay in the background." I didn't like people getting too close to me, and I didn't show much affection to my children— what was wrong with that? I thought that was normal because kids are not always loveable anyway, especially when they start walking and talking. The truth was that I had altered my behavior to fit my own personal circumstances so that I could survive. It had nothing to do with God. I had created a new thing in myself. It was my juvenile way of survival.

But I definitely believe that God was with me throughout all that I endured. I believe that God was the reason why I did not lose my mind. I believe that God was the reason why I did not succumb to my circumstances totally and abuse other children or become a promiscuous person. I believe that God is the reason why I didn't hate all men and put them in one horrible category. I could have turned to women for comfort sexually as well as emotionally.

I thank God that I chose not to be a product of my environment! I realized the wrong that was displayed and done to me, and I decided to do some things differently. That was definitely

THANK GOD FOR CAMOUFLAGE

God keeping His hands on my life even when I thought I was alone!

Session VI: I was feeling better about the sessions, and I was not even concerned if others knew about it. Our sessions were at our outreach center, and sometimes other people would be there, but I was developing a little boldness, and I was okay with it. I was sure that they had some issues of their own. It's better to deal with my issues rather than slack off in areas where God has called me to be. People will talk whether I am dealing with issues or not, so I would just focus on being healed.

It was obvious that the enemy had found out that I was at a weak point in my life because, whenever I would experience progress, a lot of more pressing challenges would crop up to frustrate me and make healing more difficult so that I just wanted to give up. I was so tired of fighting for my sanity!

Once we got into this session, I discovered that there hadn't been a time when I had been overjoyed in my life. There hadn't been a time when I could say, "That was the happiest day of my life." I tried so hard to think back and find something, but I just couldn't recall anything. I didn't remember childhood birthday parties or being taken to a park. I didn't remember my parents hugging me and displaying affection, validating me and affirming me. I had none of that!

Nothing exciting happened during elementary and junior high school. During my senior year of high school, the most exciting thing that happened to me was getting pregnant and having to get an abortion. I remember having to borrow money from my Mom to get that abortion, and the saddest thing about it was that no one acknowledged the condition I was in before, during, or after I received the abortion. No one acknowledged how traumatizing it was emotionally and physically to have a child ripped out of you in pieces. Everyone was just glad it was over so that I could get prepared for college. Surely I didn't want to embarrass the family.

It was a very painful procedure, and I was moving very slowly afterwards, and I remember being left behind and not even helped to get inside the car. I don't even think the other guilty party even told his family. The most he did was to pay my Mom her money back for the procedure.

I remember when my parents and I had to sign papers for college because I had received a partial scholarship for Track and Field to the University of Alabama. I remember thinking that neither of my parents had ever been to one track meet in the four years that I had thrown the shot put and discus. I was always in the newspaper, and I had broken several records for distance thrown, and yet they had no idea what that scholarship was for. My parents had not supported me throughout high school at all, so that time was not as happy for me as it should have been. I focused on the negative because I didn't know any better

I think about all of the positive energy and attention that I received in high school, all of the track meets and state meets where I had come in first place, and I was such a sad person. I could never be happy for myself. I always thought I could do better. I remember a particular track meet at which I had come in first place. I knew that I could have thrown farther than I did, but I still came in first place. I remember walking out into the field, wanting to be alone, and crying like a baby, as if I had come in last! People thought I was crazy. There is no place before first place, so what was my problem?

I expected more from myself than Jesus did. I guess I thought I could be perfect; surely that would have made up for the jacked-up childhood I endured.

It is so important to deal with the issues that come into our lives because unresolved issues will fill us up and spill over into everything we do. They will not just go away! They have to be dealt with, and you have to overcome them in order to successfully proceed in life. Issues will continue to pile up with other issues until we decide to handle them, and, the longer you wait, the more you have to handle. You will have to dig out the new issues to get to the root cause.

I thought about when I left college and ran off to get married to the person who had impregnated me in high school. (How smart was that?) A lot of questions went through my mind as I was dropping out of college. *What will my parents think of me now? Are we really ready for this? Will our relationship last? Do I think this is the only way to keep this boy in my life? If I choose to finish my education, will he wait for me?* These were all unanswered questions and definitely reasons why I should have kept my butt in school. If you have that many questions about a life-changing decision, you more than likely should not do it. I decided to do it anyway; love would conquer all.

I flew to Hawaii and we got married in the backyard of one of the judge's homes. Shortly after marriage, I got pregnant. Having the baby was not an exciting time because I almost died giving birth to her, and then she was born with medical problems. My husband was not much help at all because he was too busy running the streets and sharing himself with other women. I was alone in Hawaii with my first child who was sick, and I was having marital problems with my husband. This was not a part of the plan, I needed more cooperation in my young life!

I was separated and divorced within two and a half years. It was a waste of my educated time, and now I had to go back home and face the music with a baby. I was definitely not happy!

I thought about my second marriage. We were married at the court house in Ohio. It was very impersonal. We exchanged our vows in the corner of the hallway by the front door. Since we did not bring a witness, a stranger who had just walked in the door of the court house agreed to witness and sign our marriage license. I really had a different idea about how this would take place. I thought there would be an elderly lady to escort us into this little personal and decorated room. I figured she would play a lovely selection on the piano and her elderly husband would marry us; surely I had been watching too much television again! I cried so much on that day, causing my husband to think I didn't want to be married to him. Besides that, we had been living together for almost a year, and I knew that was wrong. Mom did teach me not to shack up with a man. She would say that, if I was good enough to live with, then I was good enough to marry! Getting married was just the right thing to do. There was no formal proposal; we just decided one day to get married because it was better than living in sin!

I recalled having my second child and I started having complications early in the pregnancy. My baby ended up coming too soon and only weighed one-and-half pounds. Within three-and-a-half weeks, her lungs collapsed, and she had open heart surgery. We had several close calls within that time and we were running back and forth to the hospital. She eventually got tired and passed away. She was definitely a little fighter like her mom. We buried her on October 4, 1990. Although it was a sad and challenging time in my life, I was somewhat relieved when she passed on because she went through so much and she was so tiny. We had to buy doll clothes to bury her in.

Prior to her death, the doctors and nurses were poking and prodding her daily, and they had several machines attached to her. There were tubes coming from several parts of her tiny body. It was devastating to see! I will never forget the day she died. The nurse disconnected all of the machines, wrapped her up in a blanket, and brought her to me. I remember her little body still being warm, and a calm came over me. I cuddled her and rubbed her little head knowing that she was innocent and in God's hands, resting in that perfect peace. The moment was very intense. The nurse let me hold her as long as I wanted, and then she came and took her away. The next time I saw her, she was in that tiny

THANK GOD FOR CAMOUFLAGE

casket at the funeral home. I hoped I'd never have to experience that again!

My thinking was that I had to suffer like that because I had that abortion in high school. I just knew this was my punishment! I was challenged with all that I had endured up to that point and that was what I came up. Somebody should have schooled a sister on Life 101!

Now that my husband's one-and-only blood child had passed on, I really wanted to give him another child. I struggled to get pregnant again and had many failed attempts. Everything inside my body was in an uproar; I really just needed to relax! When I finally decided that one was plenty and my husband would just have to love his step child as his own, that's when I got pregnant again. Complications were inevitable at that point. I was only about eight weeks along when problems arose.

After two previous emergency C-Sections, my cervix proved to be too weak to carry full term. The doctors stitched up my cervix, and I was on bed rest for about six months. I solved a lot of crossword puzzles and watched a lot of T.V. Finally, my youngest child was born, C-Section #3, and, as soon as I received the okay that she was a healthy baby girl, I immediately had my tubes tied, clipped and burned. I remember wanting to remove them myself!

The only thing that I felt proud of was that I was married both times I had children (excluding the abortion) and that my present husband was not sharing himself with another woman—as far as I knew, anyhow. He seemed to genuinely love me and the girls, but I still had to watch him because he was a man. Both of us needed help with spiritual matters, but we respected one another, and we had decided that divorce was not an option. We tried hard not to allow anything to come between us.

I was not married when I was first impregnated, but no one knew about the abortion, so it became just another addition to my childhood secrets. I would pretend that I did all the right things in my life. I didn't even talk to the Lord about that one. I was still running the show, thinking I had total control of my life. I could not possibly bother the Lord with stuff like that; He was too busy.

After skimming over the events of my lifetime, I came to the conclusion that I never "allowed" myself to be happy. I had determined that the sexual abuse that I had endured as a child meant that something was wrong with me, and how dare I attempt to be happy about anything! I chose to look at every glass as being half empty. I focused on the negative in everything and always tried to make myself responsible for it in some way.

From the beginning, I knew that it was not my fault because I knew no other way. My gods (parents) had failed me. I never thought the abuse was right, and I ended up blaming myself because everyone else seemed to be blameless. They did not even get a slap on the wrist, but now that I know another way, being connected to a God that faileth not, I now know that a person makes a choice to see the glass as half empty. I know now that God can make what we think is a bad situation into something good. I know now that no weapon formed against me shall prosper. I now know that, by His stripes, I am already healed. I now know that, if I wait upon the Lord, He will renew my strength. I now know that I have been rescued from the domain of the enemy and transferred into the kingdom of Christ and redeemed by His blood. My flesh is diminishing daily as I allow the Holy Spirit to manifest Himself from the inside out. Needless to say, after this session, I was advised to seek scriptures about joy.

~INNER HEALING II~

Session VII: It had been two weeks since the last session, and I was okay. The enemy was still coming at me in every direction, but I didn't seem to be so scared. I was learning to keep my whole armor of God on and roll with the punches. I was still battling with wanting the minister to hold my hand through it all, but that too would pass. I was determined to continue to move forward.

I had finally found a safe place to go when times got hard. The Lord gave me a vision of a very tall glass skyscraper. It was so tall that you could not see the top of it.

The skyscraper was soundproof and very peaceful on the inside. The vision was of me lying on the inside at the bottom of the skyscraper in a fetal position. It seemed as though a tornado was in motion on the outside. Debris was flying everywhere, and it was starting to pile up around me on the outside of the skyscraper. I realized that the debris was blocking my vision. I couldn't see what was going on anymore. The Lord lifted me up above the debris, and I was able to see again. The higher the debris piled up, the higher the Lord lifted me above it. There was chaos and destruction going on all around me, but it did not affect me; it could not touch me. I was having peace in the eye of a storm. The Lord surrounded me with His protection and kept me safe until the storm passed over.

The Lord was showing me that He was bigger than anything that I could ever go through. He was showing me that the skyscraper was His arms around me, and the fact that I could not see the top meant that there is no limit to what He could do for me. It was far beyond what I could ever envision. He showed me that, although I would experience rough times, I could move forward in the midst of them. I can be safe in His arms as He carries me through adversity.

Sometimes I would try to go back to that place and feel the embrace of the Lord. I wanted to just bask in His glory. A friend of mine reminded me that I didn't need to go back, because I was already there. The vision was brought to me to show me where I was and not where I was headed. The Lord was protecting me right then as I was going through the storm. That was so powerful to me! I was in great expectation of what was to come in the near future.

Periodically, I would bring gifts to the minister to make me feel better about taking up her time, so we talked about why I give. She even asked me to stop bringing gifts until I could give clarity on why I give.

I was trying not to be offended because I knew it was a choice to be offended. I thought she was trying to strip me of my last ounce of dignity. She was even trying to take away the little bit of pride that I had left. I guess I was supposed to have total cleansing and total healing; however, I only wanted to get just enough to maintain my sanity.

I wasn't trying to soar with my eagle wings. I just wanted to walk upright, and I wanted the minister to clear me out a path.

She had teamed up with the Holy Spirit, and they were really trying to get to the core of this situation. Okay, do I fight for control or just go with the flow? I didn't want any setbacks, so I told myself that I would go with the flow. I allowed her to help me as I tried to relinquish a little of that control.

I went home, and I really sought the Lord's help to answer that question. I didn't do things for people so that they would like me because that was never a major concern of mine. I had always been concerned with other people's happiness, but not to gain their friendship. I would do things for people just because it made me feel good to see other people happy. I had always wanted everyone's needs to be met. I didn't want anyone to be left without some kind

THANK GOD FOR CAMOUFLAGE

of support. I believed it was the only way that I could get a little relief from being so unhappy. I thought that I was so messed up and that there was no hope for me. However, it was not too late for someone else. I thought that maybe I could save the rest of the world. That's why I would sometimes give, even if I sacrificed my own needs or desires. I was never mad at the world for what happened to me. I wanted to protect others from going through the same thing.

I know now that I am not expected to do that. Being a part of someone else's happiness is a wonderful thing, and it's not even important to be acknowledged in the giving. I have never craved attention in that way. I received too much of the wrong attention as a child, so I preferred not being noticed. It just felt good for me to see that a need was met.

I believe that God has given me the spiritual gift of serving. I believe that, over the years, the enemy had turned it into something ungodly. Sometimes we allow our purpose and gifts to be distorted. We have genuine intentions that need to be redirected. There have been times when I was clearly prompted by the Holy Spirit to give something, and there have been times when my flesh wanted to save someone, totally disregarding myself and my own situation. I have learned that, just because you have knowledge of a person's need, you aren't necessarily the one to provide that need. It is very important to be able to hear from the Lord before you do anything because there are other voices that can prompt you as well, and they are not of God! We can be deceived so easily sometimes.

I am reminded of a time when I had a trying day and I was on an emotional rollercoaster. I was sharing with the minister along my journey in great detail. I was a bit disappointed that I didn't get a phone call later that day from her to check on me. Now that I had totally exposed all of my life secrets, I needed her to be there until the end. I remember her telling me that she wanted to call but purposely didn't because I needed to be drawing closer to God and not to her. Well, I was not appreciative of all of her self control at the time because my life was spiraling out of control! I realized later that it was definitely the right thing to do. I was depending on the minister so much that I could imagine it being very draining for her. I guess somebody needed to consistently follow the Holy Spirit because I wasn't doing it at that time.

One of the saddest things about my life was that I had never valued my self worth. It was always very easy to put others before me, even people who were not significant in my life— people who didn't care much about me at all. I was always good at hurting myself while trying to do the right thing for others. I guess, in some sick way, I thought it was better than allowing others to hurt me. I didn't set out to purposely hurt myself, but it always ended up that way. I'm sure that it was a subconscious matter.

The enemy is smooth. He will sneak in and have you self destructing before you know it. To have balance is a daily struggle because it's just as bad to be excessive about what we consider to be good things as it is to be excessive about bad things. We have been taught that it is better to give than to receive and what goes around comes around. I have always thought that, when you give, it will come back to you, at whatever cost endured. I didn't realize that I am joint heirs with Christ Jesus. My blessings come directly from Him. I didn't realize that God loves me so much that He gave His only son to be crucified on my behalf. His desire is that I prosper as my soul prospers. He does not want me to suffer with the spirit of lack. God wants me to be obedient to His word so that He can bless me with more than enough, and then I can bless others with my overflow, and it will not affect my circumstances! We have to die to flesh daily and become more spiritual beings so that we can be clean vessels used by the Holy Spirit.

Session VIII: I was managing much better before the sessions. (Previously, I would be sitting around, watching the clock, and being very anxious.) But things were really winding down now; I realized that this might be the last session. Even though I didn't think I was ready to end it, I was challenged with accepting it.

The session started, and I voiced my opinion about being released. I started asking questions like, "How do you know when it is time to release someone?" I was questioning her ministry and trying to indirectly let her know that I was not ready to be released. Had she run out of exercises for me? Was session eight magical in some way, or was that all she was willing to commit to? Was she just tired of me? Did I even have a say in the matter?

Normally I think we give the enemy too much credit, but I must say that he is on his job 25 hours a day, eight days a week, seeking to destroy anyone who is vulnerable enough to be overcome by him. He will swarm around you until you fall short and allow him an entry way into your life. One of his main weapons is fear, and it will definitely master you if you are not careful. We have to watch and pray at all times!

Now that the minister wanted to push me out of the nest to fly on my own, I was questioning her authority. I felt that we needed to be of one accord in this thing. Was the Lord telling her to release me, but had He forgotten to tell me, or was I just not trying to hear the Lord

THANK GOD FOR CAMOUFLAGE

right then? I could not comprehend being released at that time. How could she just cut me loose like that? I thought we had developed a friendship. I was disappointed and feeling quite abandoned. I felt I had been to that place before: being left behind.

Paranoia had obviously set in. I was definitely seeing straight jackets in the near future. Before this session, I would have told anybody how much stronger I was in the Lord. I would have told them how I was ready to fly on my own, that all I needed was Jesus under my wings. This was all true, but I lacked confidence in myself. I knew all the right things to say, but, when the time came to do them, the story would quickly change.

A minister who had been delivered from homosexuality had come to our church. He made a statement that changed my life that day. He said," If there is anything in your past that still haunts you today, is it really in your past?" It made me realize that I needed to deal with being sexually abused. I had been nurturing that abuse as if it was a baby, and it had definitely grown past its due date—years past its due date. That was a turning point for me; I needed to hear that.

However, still sitting in session eight, I was trying to plead my case. Out of pity, I was sure, the minister decided to allow me a little more time to come to my senses. She gave me the task of seeking the Holy Spirit for guidance in finding a confidant—a friend to share with when I needed to share. She explained to me on more than one occasion that she was not available to be a friend to me outside of counseling. Well, I guess I was not showing myself to be too friendly at that point, but I mustered enough pride to receive what she said with no problem. I only saw her as my counselor, and I knew I was only showing myself to be needy and fragile when I was in sessions with her. I didn't think that I could be friends with her, anyway. The information I revealed in our sessions together would possibly affect any outside friendship with the minister. *I'll leave that alone*, I thought. I would always look at her as a minister and choir director—and she would probably always look at me as one of the biggest challenges of her life.

I needed to figure out what I was going to do when my sessions were over.

I was thinking of how I had nakedly exposed myself emotionally. I thought about how broken and torn I had been. I really felt that I was being prematurely left to fend for myself before I was ready. I thought I would be prepared for such a time as this, but I truly didn't feel that I was.

Now that the violins had stopped playing my sad song, "Woe is Me," I really needed to realize that the minister was not my source. I

THANK GOD FOR CAMOUFLAGE

still had not gotten it. If it were up to me to determine when counseling should stop, I would still be there now. It was hard stepping into unfamiliar territory. You want to be equipped and have insight into what you are going into. Sometimes we are ready and we do not even know it, and that is why God appoints those to be used by Him to lead us.

All those years I thought I was in control, and now I was running scared; not knowing which direction to go. I still had a lot to learn.

Session IX: Before this session, I was still trying to come to grips with the fact that our sessions would be ending, and it wasn't getting easier. I felt as if my intellect and maturity had been stripped away while I was facing this major flaw in my life. I had totally lost my ability to keep my composure. I used to have major skills at camouflaging imperfections—now, I was losing it!

During this session, we elaborated more on why I was so comfortable serving and giving to others but had a hard time receiving.

As a child, I received so many negative things, emotionally and physically. As an adult, I wanted to be in control of receiving to evaluate whether or not it was good. To keep from having to evaluate people's motives, I just decided that I would not take anything from anyone. I would do all of the giving, and that way I could know that the giving was going to be a good thing, with good motives. My giving would be from the heart! When you are receiving, you never know if it is going to be good or bad; you don't know if strings will be attached, so I thought I was in control by not receiving at all. It prevents having to receive bad things. You can get to the point when you don't think you are worthy of receiving good things and think that everyone is out to hurt you in some way.

Since I had never dealt with my childhood issues, I could only relate to them with a childlike mentality. I had to go back there, even as an adult. I believe that was the reason why I latched on to the minister so quickly during our sessions. I was definitely in a childlike state when I started these sessions, and the minister became the parent that I never had. Finally someone cared enough to love and protect me from those people who were hurting me.

I never thought I had anyone to protect me as a little girl. It seemed as though time was frozen while I failed in several attempts at trying to run things—then along came the minister. I latched on to her like the Jaws of Life! I'm sure that she naturally wanted to run away from me but, when we're being led by the Holy Spirit, we have to reluctantly endure some things that we would not endure on our own. I didn't want to be left alone again. I had literally immersed myself in the relationship as we counseled. I felt as if I had a split personality. I was experiencing my issues as a child; as if that part of my life was frozen in time, but I was also trying to be a Christ-like adult ministering to others and longing for God's approval.

After each session, I was usually embarrassed by something that I said or did during my time with the minister, but that was okay, I knew I would get it together soon. I thought I would be in this process for as long as I existed. I knew that I would not be perfected until I left this earth and entered into the spirit realm, but I was determined to be a functional and productive Christian in ministry.

I continued to struggle with finding a friend whom I thought I could trust, and it became obvious that I was the reason why I hadn't. I had already allowed the minister into my little world, and that was plenty for me. This transparency thing was for the birds, especially since I had been solo for so long.

I had a couple more sessions to go, and I could not express how much I appreciated the minister's assistance. I had a hard time expressing myself on several occasions because I believe that, when you know where you are emotionally, you probably should not say everything that you are feeling—simply because you are relaying emotions, and that's not always a cute presentation; actually, it can be quite ugly at times.

I always thought that, once you realize the error of your ways in life, you don't have to expose the error—just change it. I thought I could save myself lots of embarrassing moments because, once you put something out there, you can't take it back. In ministry, it is very important to be transparent (real) because of the difficulty to receive from those who act as though they have had the perfect Christian walk with no challenges. People need to know that you can relate to what they are going through. They want to see where God has brought you from. If you are in denial and not dealing with your own issues by way of your relationship with God, then you will definitely have some embarrassing moments in life. Whatever you're keeping in the dark will eventually be revealed.

God was really dealing with me and I was trying to stay out of my own way. I had probably caused the minister to start her own book at this point, starring me. That was nothing I was proud of, actually, it was quite shameful!

Session X: A couple of weeks had gone by, and I felt I was ready to discontinue the sessions. I had planned to go in and let the minister know that I was ready to go on my own.

THANK GOD FOR CAMOUFLAGE

I was feeling strong and didn't feel I needed to depend on another person as much. Maybe the minister and I could meet quarterly to have coffee and discuss my progress. Besides, once the sessions stopped, I would have to totally depend on the Holy Spirit to guide me. I would not have any other choice. The minister did not have to push me out of the nest; I would just jump out on my own! Session ten was the end!

Okay, it didn't work out that way! I always talked a good game before the sessions were actually in session. The minister had given me a book to read and wanted me to meet with her in a couple of weeks to talk about it. Well, that was just convenient for me. The book, *Hind Feet on High Places*, was very interesting. The characters in the book represented different feelings and emotions, and I remember relating too much to the main character, "Much Afraid." I did not realize that my book had already been written before my sessions started. The minister read me very well.

This character had some obvious problems concerning her outward appearance, which naturally affected her self esteem and how she allowed people to treat her. In the place she lived, she was under the authority of the "Chief Shepherd," who was definitely symbolic of our Lord and Savior Jesus Christ. He always met her right where she was and coached her to the higher places. She shed a lot of weights as she was promoted from glory to glory. As she soared to higher heights, she had to endure the valleys and the storms of life so that she could gain more strength and faith to continue to the next level.

As she progressed to higher heights, she began to see herself as the Chief Shepherd saw her, which made her confident, and she began to build on that.

The book depicted how narrow the road is that we travel in our Christian walk. That road will not always have smooth and level terrain: as we travel, there will be valleys that will cause us to lose our reception of the Lord. There will be storms in life that will slow us down because we cannot see clearly and therefore do not know where the Lord is trying to guide us. There will be tornadoes in life that will totally take us off course and cause us to temporarily lose our way. There will be hurricanes in life that will completely wash us out, and the Lord may have to carry us for a season. We will have to constantly seek God's face so that we may fulfill our purpose in this life.

I listen to a lot of Gospel music, and most of the songs counsel us about enduring hard times, keeping the faith, holding on to God's promises, and pressing our way through all that comes against us. They can be encouraging songs that minister to people who are struggling in

THANK GOD FOR CAMOUFLAGE

some area of their life. Listening to the songs would sometimes be depressing for me also because they brought home the reality that everyone in the world was struggling with something. Life is just one big struggle, and, although we think we are alone in our struggles, such struggles are actually very common and even wide spread in some instances.

I know that sexual abuse is rampant, and is being inflicted upon people at younger and younger ages. I also know that one person cannot save the world, but there are so many people who could benefit by learning about our adversities and knowing that there is life after being sexually abused. Oprah Winfrey, Donnie McClurkin, Lee Daniels, and many others are prime examples of that. They are fortunate to be a blessing to so many lives.

It is also good for people to know that there are other people, "regular" people who have had experience with sexual abuse and can relate to their problems—people who are willing to be candid and open and risk exposing themselves to help others. This knowledge could definitely give someone hope.

If everyone would do their part and pay forward the blessings they have received, and even the adversities that they have overcome, we would definitely be on the right road toward saving the world.

It is good to know that, as Christians, who study God's word and walk in His obedience, we can have that serenity that only God can provide, and then we are allowed to shine in spite of what we face in life. We can be camouflaged by God even in the midst of going through. Thank God for camouflage!

Session XI: I really wanted to end the sessions now. I was not sure if I was ready or not, but I had developed a bit of an attitude with myself by this time! I was frustrated; whatever I had not received by then would not matter. I just wanted to get off the emotional roller-coaster ride; I was tired. If I wasn't ready to fly, I guess I would just have to crash.

I could not thoroughly convey the gratitude that I had for the minister's spirit of patience with me. She had been very gentle, caring, and consistent during every session. I was sure that I had been very instrumental in strengthening and improving the consistency of her prayer life as well. I know that I challenged her!

For this particular session, we met at a restaurant. I thought that a neutral and public place would be great for ending the sessions as well as helping me keep my composure. God was still dealing with me on my control issue.

I had not been focused on the sessions, so I had not finished the book the minister had loaned me. The two weeks had gone by so fast. I had not even thought about finding another confidant. At that point, I was starting to become numb to it all.

It's hard being a human being! There are a lot of complicated ingredients that go into our being. I believe we can go through a lifetime and not even know ourselves totally.

I was exhausted and very upset with myself because I had agreed to another session. I wasn't sure how much I cared right then. I felt that I was slipping into a deep depression. But pride kicked in, and I was able to make it through the session and keep my composure in the restaurant the whole time; that was my goal from the start.

She gave me some extra time to finish the book, and of course that led to another session. *This is getting old*, I thought, but I managed to roll with it. I had developed the ability to roll with the punches of life so that the hits could be tolerated and not seem so powerful. I didn't want to be seen as down and out, so I just learned to roll with whatever life threw at me, and then I'd get back up and fake it some more.

Session XII: We started this session on the lower level of the building in a different room. I noticed that this particular room was closer to the exit door.

It was starting to hit me that this was really the last session. I thought we were going to our regular setting upstairs. *I'm going to be okay*, I kept telling myself. I was still feeling some embarrassment about previous sessions, previous letters, and previous phone conversations with her, but I was determined to get over it. I was wondering what our relationship would be like from that day forward, but, whatever it would be, I was going to be okay with it.

Could the minister erase all that I had exposed to her and accept me as I was? If not, I was still determined that I would be okay. That is what my mouth said, anyway. I was really trying to convince myself that I was glad about the sessions ending.

We were reviewing and having a general conversation about previous sessions. This last session didn't even last an hour. I could not believe it; it was finally going to be over! I didn't even have time to think of an excuse to continue. Although I am a large-framed woman, I quickly realized that I had to be a "big girl" in a whole different sense now.

We talked a little about being bound, relinquishing control to God, and allowing Him to use me. I wanted to be completely open with

THANK GOD FOR CAMOUFLAGE

God and receive my breakthrough. I had been so busy trying to hide things throughout life. I was not free to be the person God created me to be. If I could be free enough to open up to the minister and trust that God was leading her, surely I should have been able to open up to the same God who created me: the one who would give me grace and not condemn me; the one who would forget all of my ungodly behavior and give me a clean slate, the one who would look at me as a new creation and not hold my past against me. I could not understand why that was so difficult for me!

The last session was over, and no other sessions were scheduled. I was actually walking out of the door. I was in the car, and I did not even know where I was going.

I probably could have gotten an award for my performance, but reality was setting in and I became very distraught. I tried to get myself together long enough to get out of the driveway. I could not let the minister see me sitting there in the midst of a serious breakdown. I was really suffering and feeling so alone. I still had not completely realized that God had been with me the whole time. I was not in the mindset of spiritual things. I was focused on that actual person who had come to my rescue—but how much could I impose on one person? I was sure that the minister was ready to retire after dealing with me. I had to work it out, me and the Holy Spirit.

I drove away in the most pitiful state. At that point, I realized that healing had just started. My sessions had been like military boot camp. I was in training on how to combat the wars of life, and then I was sent to battle. I know that the Holy Spirit was with me because I was so zoned out that I didn't even remember the drive home. I really had a hard time giving in to a lot of feelings that I was experiencing. At that point, I had had my share of breakdowns. After the fact, I realized that my feelings had to be exposed and dealt with, just as issues do. I thought I had exposed too much already, so, once again, I was trying to have some control. I thought I had to keep a little pride in my back pocket.

God was revealing me to me. I started realizing how much I had accomplished and how further accomplishment would be a continual process. Focus on the positive, I said.

THANK GOD FOR CAMOUFLAGE

~YET HOLDING ON~

It was the day after my last session. It was becoming even clearer to me that I was the one in the way of my progress. I made it through the day, and I knew that time would make life a little easier. I just wanted time to go a lot faster.

I was moving along just fine. I was trying to become one with the fact that I needed to become a more spiritual being. I had to know that God was with me even if I could not see or touch Him. I had to know that God could provide so much more than any human being could even offer. I hoped the minister was still praying for me. I knew where I needed to be, but I struggled to get there.

It had been two weeks, and I would normally be heading to my next session. Suddenly I was reminded that there were no more sessions. What was I going to do?

The Holy Spirit became my source of hope and helped me to get through the rough days. I wanted to call the minister on several occasions, but I restrained myself, and I got through it. I had to really believe that God would not put more on me than I could bear, no matter what it felt like, because I felt as if He had dropped a ton of bricks on me!

It was Thanksgiving, and I was having a pity party. I guess I was not thankful enough for all the turkey and other food that I had consumed. I was going through some changes, and I broke down and called the minister. I really did not want to spoil her day. I was actually surprised that she answered my call after what I'd put her through. I really had expected to get her answering service, but she answered. It would have been so much easier if I had gotten the answering service.

Anyway, when she answered the phone, pride kicked in. and I expressed to her that I was thinking about her and just wanted to say "Happy Thanksgiving." (I basically lied.) The conversation was short. After it ended, I had my little crying spell and moved on. I guess I thought that hearing her voice would cheer me up, but it really caused a minor setback. Nevertheless, I sometimes found excuses to call her anyway. I think I was my worst enemy at times. I had mastered self abuse at that point.

Anyway, I got through a few months, and I thought I was getting somewhere. Suddenly I started having dreams that my Uncle and Father were coming back from the dead and coming after me again. In my dream, we were at their funeral, and I remember the people in the church acting as if it were normal for them to get up out of the casket and live again. I was the only one running scared. I thought everyone was crazy except me. I was one scared sister when I woke up. Somehow I ended up being under my husband without waking him up. For a while I was fearful of sleeping at night. I was having some struggles. I was contemplating taking drugs so that I could sleep. I felt that I needed to rest beyond dreaming. I thought that maybe I could get a hold of some anesthesia or something similar.

I continued being attacked in my dreams. I broke down again and called the minister on a Friday. I did not act desperate because I was a big girl, and I was claiming my healing. I asked the minister if she could meet with me on Monday, which was a day off for me. Thank God discernment kicked in on her part, and she offered to meet me at a restaurant the very next morning before work. I knew that I would have struggled unnecessarily had I waited until Monday, but I guess I figured that I had made it that far; why not be tortured a few more days?

It had to be difficult for the minister to try and figure out when I really needed her and when I was being prideful. You have to make your request known so that someone can assist you! I knew what the word of God said, but I struggled to walk in it.

Anyway, she brought to my attention that I was not being aggressive enough with my prayers at bedtime. I allowed the enemy entrance when I did not prepare to be spiritually covered while I slept. I received that advice and implemented it before going to bed.

God is truly good at all times, and in time He definitely heals wounds. I had been proceeding quite well without the minister being so available to me. The Holy Spirit and I were becoming one, and as I became a more spiritual being, I didn't need tangible assistance so much. Still, I try to always be mindful that we are here for one another. God did not place us here to be so independent, prideful, and never needing anyone.

I can't afford to go backwards spiritually because I would not want to do an injustice to others in my position. Surely there is more that is required of me now. It is time to step up and move to higher places.

My motto has changed from "Thank God for Camouflage" to "Keep it Real." We need to keep it real with God and everyone else who comes in contact with us. If we are not being real, people will only know what we outwardly portray as we slowly die on the inside. Now, sometimes a little camouflaging is necessary when we face some challenges in life. We can't walk around looking so downcast from the negative situations we may be experiencing, because we wouldn't be representing our Father

THANK GOD FOR CAMOUFLAGE

very well if we did that. We have to learn to keep our heads up even in the midst of trials and tribulations. I believe that God will automatically camouflage our issues when we follow His lead.

God can mold us and heal us so much faster when we submit to Him and not resist Him.

He is all-knowing, so He knows our struggles; however, He wants us to be honest with ourselves. We cannot allow the spirit of denial to hinder our progress in life. When God is in control, we can get through adversities without being consumed. When we choose to stand on God's word, we won't fall for everything!

~A PERSONAL WORST~

A personal worst is the most difficult thing that *you* have ever had to confront and conquer in *your* life. It has nothing to do with anyone else's life and should not be compared to anyone else's personal worst. A personal worst is something that you would not wish on anyone—that is, if you have a Christ-Like spirit.

While enduring a sexual-abuse ordeal, I became very sensitive to what people would say and how they thought about certain issues. A lot of people have strong opinions about their perspective on life situations and must struggle to meet you where *you* are in *your* life.

Many people find it hard to embrace the differences that we have; they can't understand why you do the things you do or why you say the things you say or even why you believe the things you believe. Who are we to question God's work? He purposely made us different and we need to exercise more acceptances in that area.

I believe that people minimize your situation or circumstance because they either can't relate to what you are going through or they think that their situation or circumstance is worse than yours. Because of that, people do not

THANK GOD FOR CAMOUFLAGE

seem to understand why you struggle to get through a particular situation because surely they have gone through something worse than you.

People who do not deal with their issues will lead very lonely and unhappy lives. Issues will consume your whole life if you allow the enemy to keep you in darkness about it. Even when we push issues so far to the back of our minds that we think we have forgotten them, they will subconsciously continue to affect our lives and have us believing that our actions are just because of the way God made us. Issues take you out of your comfort zone and can make you feel as if you are losing your mind. You will be deceived into believing that you are not worthy of God's love or forgiveness, even if you had no control over what happened to you. It is so sad to know that people actually pass through this life having never dealt with their issues.

Your personal worst issues are even harder to deal with when you try to share them with others who want to categorize how your particular issue rates. They want to tell you how you should be responding to it and how long it should take you to get over it. I do understand that social scientists have done research on people and decided what is healthy and normal and what is unhealthy and abnormal. They have studied a particular number of people in particular areas and come up with an average healing time. Maybe they study people in big cities where the cost of living is high and lots of traffic and tourists cause higher levels of stress. Maybe they study poor areas about which outsiders have fewer concerns but where the inhabitants have a shorter response time for those wreaking havoc in their lives. The bottom line is that problems in life are handled differently. Ten people can have a variation of responses to the same problem and take different periods of time to resolve that problem.

Often, we are told to go to the hospitals and nursing homes and visit some people with *real* issues. Sometimes our elders in these places will tell us to just keep on living, that there is a lot more to come. They will tell us about the days when they picked cotton and how they were treated so badly. They will tell us about how they had to walk miles to school and how they suffered from so much lack. They say that they were made very strong because of it.

Well, I'm sure that, had I lived back in those days, a thing like that would have been a personal worst for me, and it could only make me a better and stronger person as well. From my experience with elderly people, I find a lot of bitterness in them because a lot of them are still bound and have secrets that they do not talk about—secrets that they will take to their graves

THANK GOD FOR CAMOUFLAGE

because they believe that they are too old to resolve them. A lot of elderly people are mad at the world because they have not lived to their fullest capacity and now feel that it's too late for them. They have chosen to be a product of what they were taught and how they were made to feel and then make everyone around them take the blame for it. From my perspective, that is exchanging one place of bondage for another. I believe that, as long as you have breath in your body, it's not too late to make changes and live a free life as God intended. I, personally, would rather have my last days on this earth be free from bondage and open to the things of God. I want to be a clean vessel for the Lord, willing and able to be used by Him. That's just my personal opinion.

We are often told about the wars going on and how we could be wandering in the midst. I have also seen many natural disasters broadcast on television. I have observed homelessness abroad and the creative ways that we are killing each other all over the world, not to mention many other issues that I could not even imagine experiencing—and yet none of this changes my personal worst. All of those things could definitely be a temporary distraction from my situation. They would definitely take my focus away for a little while. Those issues are those people's personal worst, but that doesn't make me forget about mine. My personal worst is still my personal worst. One can have compassion and sensitivity for others who are going through turmoil. You can intercede and even feel a lot of other people's pain, but your personal worst is an individual thing. I would choose one of those other issues any day rather than the degrading experiences of being sexually defiled by my Uncle and my Father, so it depends on your perspective, but it is definitely individualized.

Issues affect people differently, and, therefore, healing times may vary. In my case, age was a factor—as was the lack of religious and family support. I had to grow spiritually and experience the true and living God for myself, and I didn't have my parents' support, so I didn't know how to get help for myself.

I believe that, no matter what a person goes through, someone somewhere has probably experienced something worse, but it is very inconsiderate to minimize someone else's personal worst—no matter what your personal opinion is.

People should be allowed to go through what they need to go through in the time that they require. That duration definitely has to be assessed situation by situation.

I remember an incident with my oldest daughter. She was complaining about having to spend $25.00 for something she needed for her car. At that time, she was in college, working at a job that paid minimum wage, and struggling to pay her car note and cell-phone bill. I said, "Girl, $25.00 is nothing, and you ought to be glad that you do not have your parents' debt."

As soon as I said it, I immediately regretted it because I realized I was totally disregarding her personal situation. I compared her situation with mine and totally diminished what she was saying and how financially strapped she felt. We were on totally different levels of lack. I was definitely not treating her the way I wanted to be treated, and I apologized right away!

The Bible clearly states that, as we live, there will be trials and tribulations, and I believe that our tests will become testimonies and ultimately cause us to be better Christians. We are here to help one another, and we should be open to the prompting of the Holy Spirit. We need to intercede for each other and always follow God's lead so that we will learn, grow, and be strengthened by our trials. This will allow us to pass on knowledge, perseverance, and endurance to help our brothers and sisters in need. I believe that we exist to assist. The whole purpose of our being is to be that Godly example to others so that people can be healed and delivered and follow us as we follow Christ. When we don't have our lives in godly order, and do not seem to want to get them in order, we could cause others to stumble and maybe even fall. Whether we want to be or not, we are our brother's and sister's keeper. Let us be held accountable for the good things that we instill in the lives of others. We will surely be accountable for the bad.

It is so important to realize that our situation will rarely be as important to others as it is to us. The ultimate goal is to take our issues to the Creator. He will come down to where we are and be an awesome comforter for us. Even if our problems are not solved right away, God is more than capable. He is the one who can give us peace and contentment for the "in the mean times" until our change comes.

For those of you who have not reached your spiritual potential, counseling with a solid, substantial human being is acceptable. You will be ready to seek God on your own before you know it.

There are many people who need others to walk with them for a few miles. They need to be led until they are spiritually independent in a particular area or maybe even in general. We are all in different places with Christ, and it can be very beneficial to others as well as to ourselves to remember from whence we came. Never mind what your carnal mind thinks about it. As Christians, being led by our spiritual minds, we

THANK GOD FOR CAMOUFLAGE

strive to live according to Christ's example. We can't go wrong when we follow God's plan, on God's timing.

With timing in mind, I really applaud the minister for releasing me when she did. It is very important to hear clearly from God. He will direct us about any decision we have to make in life. Had she not released me when she did, I probably would not have benefited from the experience as much. It is a major investment of time and spirit to minister to others, and it may require more than a person is capable or willing to give. We should always seek the Holy Spirit first. I have learned that emotions can be a distraction from really knowing which battles to choose. They can also be a distraction from having a spiritual relationship with God.

~A NEW BEGINNING~

From this day forward, I realize that being complete is a challenging undertaking. It's something that we have to work at daily. In this lifetime, I do not believe that I will experience total wholeness in every area of my life, but I do believe that I can have a form of wholeness in such a way that I can have peace and be a functional Christian in spite of the turbulence in my life. I do believe that I can have balance and be able to differentiate between the things that are of God and the excessive behaviors that we can indulge in that are not of God. I will always strive for wholeness because it will help in keeping me focused. I can have the joy of the Lord as my strength, which also helps me to get through those low times in my life. With the light of the Holy Spirit, I can be free and not allow the enemy to conquer me with the bondage of darkness. I definitely feel that that freedom represents a form of wholeness.

I have to remind myself constantly to stop trying to be in control of things because it is very easy to fall back into old habits. God wants to be the head of all that we do. He wants to be acknowledged as soon as we open our eyes in

THANK GOD FOR CAMOUFLAGE

the morning. We should thank Him for covering us throughout the night and allowing us to rest in His magnificent peace. We should always thank God for the ability to take care of our daily functions without another human being's assistance. He wants to know that we appreciate our precious existence. God is so awesome!

I have been an advocate of youth most of my adult life, and I have shared with several of them how hard it is to understand that there are so many people in the world who do not believe in God, who truly believe that humans are the highest form of intelligence in the universe. Such people believe that we have evolved from animals. I personally am amazed by that. I guess that is the beauty of being free to have your own beliefs.

I share with the youth my glory in God's strategic masterpiece: human existence. I explain to them how God designed us specifically to worship and praise Him. I share the fact that we only need oxygen, water, nourishment, and rest to be able to function. Exercise would help us to function even better. We don't have to be plugged into a socket at night to be charged for the next day. We don't depend on batteries to function. We do not need a generator to be able to move and have our being, so how can one not believe that there is a higher power? Man does not have the level of knowledge to create such a being!

God's existence surrounds us daily. We can experience it when babies are born and in the process of growing older. We experience God's existence in the changing of the seasons and the precipitation that falls from the sky. Being genuinely loved by someone who requires nothing in return, not even loving them back, makes God's existence obvious. That's Godly love; the love that I have looked for from man most of my life.

I am completing this chapter of my life and proceeding toward a new beginning. I am truly healing from the major scarring of a personal worst and resurrecting to a stronger relationship with my ultimate father in Heaven.

God continues to restore me. I am definitely a healing in the making. Daily, I have to make a conscious effort to walk in His path and maintain the spiritual healing that I have attained.

It is very difficult to maintain while trying to move forward because there will always be opposition. I am learning to spiritually multi-task as I conquer opposition. Our flesh only wants to deal with one challenge at a time, but, with God, we are able to defeat and not be defeated. He will protect us and fight our battles for us when needed.

THANK GOD FOR CAMOUFLAGE

I watched a television broadcast about addictions. People who weren't addicted were interviewed, and they thought addicts should just quit.

They failed to understand why everybody could not follow the Nike slogan and "Just do it." They had no clue about strongholds and how difficult it is to break away from addictions.

It was very scary how I could relate to so much of that broadcast. I had never been a drug addict because I had always felt the strong need to be in control of myself. If there was anything that I was aware of that could remotely control me in any way, I would stay away from it. My addictions were trying to be perfect so that I would not reveal my secret. I was addicted to over-protecting my children so that they would not experience the sadness that I carried for so many years. I was addicted to needing to be affirmed by everyone to prove that I was someone. I was addicted to pride because I could not let people know that I was lacking as a wife and a parent and needed assistance. As I sought help about the sexual abuse I had suffered, I even became addicted to the minister. I wanted her to be with me 24 hours a day. I had developed an overall addictive personality, and, had I exposed all that I was experiencing, I really would have been kicked out of counseling. I actually held some things back during that time, knowing how ridiculously I was behaving. In no way did I fit the world's conception of what was beautiful on the outside, and I was even more messed up on the inside—and yet there was no rehabilitation center that I could commit myself to. I wondered occasionally if it would have been easier to have a drug addiction. I could have had a place to stay with three meals a day. I could have had visiting hours for family and friends, and someone would have always been there when I experienced those seemingly unbearable withdrawal symptoms.

I have to be mindful daily to resist those behaviors. I still struggle with the desire to be perfect so that I can pretend that I have no issues. I have to constantly guard against over-protecting my children; I have to remind myself to allow them to be more independent and to make sure that I do not handicap them any further. I even struggle to be more affectionate toward them and not think there is anything wrong about it. I still have to control my thoughts when my husband is alone with my children. I still have to refrain from calling on the minister when life situations are weighing me down.

I'm learning to go to the one who has all the right answers. I am learning to encourage myself in the Lord and just deal, on a daily basis, with the hand that is dealt to me. Time makes it

THANK GOD FOR CAMOUFLAGE

all a bit easier, although there are triggers in life that cause you to start looking back. You start getting overwhelmed, and it stops you right in your tracks, but, in the midst of it all, you come back to the reality of it all and continue to hold on to God's unchanging hand. I have failed myself on several occasions, but God has never failed me. When I get caught up in a bad spot in life, God pulls me right on through so that I can keep moving.

There was a teaching at my church called "Just Keep Moving," and it was such a powerful message. If we would just keep moving, we would end up in a better situation. We would move through challenges and not get caught up in the many things in life that hinder our witness and cause us to be delayed in fulfilling our purpose in life. I had to learn quickly to give to God those things that I have no control over and watch Him move on my behalf. In order for us to know what those things are, we have to study God's word (the Holy Bible) so that we can walk in His likeness.

Again I say that my healing process started once my sessions were over. The sessions were what I needed to get me to where I am. Being so immature about the subject at hand, I really needed a godly person to get me started in the right direction because I had no ability to utilize the Holy Spirit to help me overcome what

I felt because of the sexual abuse. I was mentally stuck at age ten in this area.

Now that the minister is no longer a crutch, I am drawing closer to God and becoming a stronger, more spiritual individual. I am becoming more equipped to be able to prevent others from taking such a matter into their own hands. I am working toward helping young people deal with the issues that arise in their lives, in order to help them have more fulfilling lives as adults.

I want to be effective in my teaching. Although the gift that I have to teach may not be the greatest, I know that it can be cultivated and effective enough to be used in a great way. I am very open to educating myself and being available to prevent many young people from unnecessary struggles. I want to teach people to not allow those mountains in life to overtake them and miss out on their godly purpose.

Incest, molestation, pedophilia, rape, etc., are sexual abuses visited upon too many people who have to endure them silently. They are taboo issues that are hidden in the souls of a very large number of God's children. Why do we keep allowing the enemy to win by choosing to stay in darkness? Darkness is the enemy's territory. God is light. The enemy cannot have anything to hold over our heads as long as we keep it real with

God. We need to expose the enemy every chance we get.

Exposure is very difficult but very necessary, especially in ministry. It is hard to penetrate someone's heart when you pretend to have lived a perfect life. People in need want to know that you have experienced some adversity, and they want to know how you survived. People want to know that you have something personal to offer, and that what you offer isn't coming from a conversation you have had with someone else or a book you have read. People want to be able to relate and be comfortable enough to know that they will not be judged.

It is really not easy to sacrifice yourself to help others because there will be judgment, and there will be some resistance. There may even be some people who choose to take offense, but, if we stay on course, God will turn it all around for our good and for His glory. It is a small price to pay when it is compared to the price that was paid for us.

We have to follow the prompting of the Holy Spirit and any conflict that it may cause will be resolved by allowing God to work it out for us.

Don't allow the enemy to reign over your life and keep you from experiencing God's promises. We have the power to speak to adversity in our lives, and it has no other choice but to leave. We have to tap into and utilize the power that has already been given to us. It is time to experience the signs and wonders of God's power within us. We are capable of performing the same miracles that Jesus did when He walked the earth in the flesh.

I really want to let go and let God! I want to be used in a mighty way! I don't want to be bound anymore! I want to feel free to praise and worship the Lord like never before!

It was challenging to even type those last statements because I know that more attacks from the enemy will come after announcing that I am a willing vessel, but fear has consumed me for far too many years. I will have to keep my vision of the skyscraper in mind because God is able to raise me above all that come against me so that I may see clearly how to continue on the path with Him.

To God be the glory for all that He is and all that He is doing in my life.

THANK GOD FOR CAMOUFLAGE

~CONCLUSION~

Sexual abuse comes in several forms, and is the type of crime that most often goes unreported. Some sexual-abuse acts can end up causing the victim's death. I believe the worst-case scenario is when the sexual abuse you suffer causes the murder of your soul—when you walk around half dead, wishing you were totally dead. You are no longer a total being; you are incomplete and acting it out wherever you go.

It is like an infectious disease, and it infects all who come in contact with you. If this is something that you are aware of, surely you want a cure for it. You don't want to infect those that you love; misleading them the way you were misled. We all want to be godly examples and treat others the way we want to be treated. God will honor that, and He will fight for you when you lack the strength that you need, and then He will strengthen you to fight for someone else in need.

Sexual abuse of daughters by a father or stepfather is the most common form of incest that is reported. Eighty percent of girls and women who were raped were victimized by someone whom they knew. That statistic comes from *reported* rapes. Imagine the percentage of the ones that go unreported. Unreported incidents do not help you or anyone else. Neither of my incidents was reported to anyone in law enforcement, and all of my subsequent struggles caused others to struggle. I want us to end those generational curses that cause us to stay in darkness. We can be free from the enemy's camp.

Statistics

Based on child-abuse information posted on the Childhelp website:
(http://www.childhelp.org/resources/learning-center/statistics).

Note: These statistics are from reported incidents of sexual abuse. So many go unreported!

- A report of child abuse is made every ten seconds.
- Ninety percent of child-sexual-abuse victims know the perpetrator in some way; 68% are abused by family members.
- Child abuse occurs at every socio-economic level, across ethnic and cultural lines, within all religions and at all levels of education.
- Thirty-one percent of women in prison in the United States were abused as children.

- Over 60% of people in drug-rehabilitation centers report being abused or neglected as a child.
- About 30% of abused and neglected children will later abuse their own children, continuing the horrible cycle of abuse.
- About 80% of 21 year olds that were abused as children met criteria for at least one psychological disorder.
- The estimated annual cost resulting from child abuse and neglect in the United States for 2007 is $104 billion.

Consequences of Child Abuse and Neglect in the USA

- Abused children are 25% more likely to experience teen pregnancy
- Children who experience child abuse and neglect are 59% more likely to be arrested as juvenile offenders, 28% more likely to be arrested as adult offenders, and 30% more likely to commit violent crimes.
- Children who have been sexually abused are 2.5 times more likely to develop alcohol abuse
- Children who have been sexually abused are 3.8 times more likely to develop drug addiction

Conclusion

- Nearly two-thirds of the people in treatment for drug abuse reported being abused as children

National Child Abuse Hotline: 1-800-444-4453

Based on information posted on the Darkness to Light website:
(http://www.darkness2light.org/KnowAbout/statistics_2.asp)

The statistics are shocking.

- One in four girls is sexually abused before the age of 18.
- One in six boys is sexually abused before the age of 18.
- One in five children is solicited sexually while on the internet.
- Nearly 70% of all reported sexual assaults (including assaults on adults) occur to children ages 17 and under.
- An estimated 39 million survivors of childhood sexual abuse exist in America today.

Even within the walls of their own homes, children are at risk for sexual abuse:

THANK GOD FOR CAMOUFLAGE

- Thirty to 40% of victims are abused by a family member.
- Another 50% are abused by someone outside of the family whom they know and trust.
- Approximately 40% are abused by older or larger children whom they know.
- Therefore, only 10% are abused by strangers.

Sexual abuse can occur at all ages, probably younger than you think:

- The median age for reported abuse is nine years old.
- More than 20% of children are sexually abused before the age of 8.
- Nearly 50% of all victims of forcible sodomy, sexual assault with an object, and forcible fondling are children under 12.

Most children don't tell even if they have been asked:

- Evidence that a child has been sexually abused is not always obvious, and many children do not report that they have been abused.
- Over 30% of victims never disclose the experience to ANYONE.
- Young victims may not recognize their victimization as sexual abuse.

Conclusion

- Almost 80% initially deny abuse or are tentative in disclosing. Of those who do disclose, approximately 75% disclose accidentally. Additionally, of those who do disclose, more than 20% eventually recant even though the abuse occurred.
- Fabricated sexual abuse reports constitute only 1% to 4% of all reported cases. Of these reports, 75% are falsely reported by adults and 25% are reported by children. Children only fabricate 0.5% of the time.

THANK GOD FOR CAMOUFLAGE

~ABOUT THE AUTHOR~

Sharon D. Campbell is a born-again Christian who has found it of the utmost importance to share her past with today's readers. She shares a story that had been hidden in her heart for such a time as this. It is Sharon's hope that this book will encourage readers to seek God's word and know that He has an answer for every situation and a plan for their lives. It is also her hope that the words on these pages will encourage others to reach the fullest potential in their lives and bring to the surface what they already have inside for the sake of future. Sharon has overcome many challenges throughout her Christian walk and shares a wealth of insight and knowledge.

Sharon wears many hats: she is a wife (married 21 years to Kenneth Campbell), a mother of two daughters (Quayeria M. Batson-Rushing and Kiera C. Campbell, ages 25 and 17, respectively), a sanitation worker at a GM facility, and a licensed nail technician. Sharon enjoys working with her hands, creating or enhancing what already exists, as exhibited in her hobbies of baking and jewelry designing.

At her church, Sharon serves as Youth Director, a member of the choir ministry, and a committee member of the "Covenant Keepers" Marriage Ministry. She enjoys observing and learning from others, experiencing the diversity of others, and she appreciates the creativity of the Creator.

LaVergne, TN USA
03 May 2010
181401LV00001B/3/P